By the same author:

DINE OUT AND LOSE WEIGHT
EAT YOURSELF SLIM...AND STAY SLIM!
THE MONTIGNAC METHOD JUST FOR WOMEN
MONTIGNAC PROVENÇAL COOKBOOK
THE MIRACLE OF WINE
EAT WELL & STAY YOUNG

Useful address:
MONTIGNAC FOOD BOUTIQUE,
CAFE & RESTAURANT
160 Old Brompton Road
LONDON SW5 0BA

Phone/Fax: 020 7370 2010
http/www.montignac.co.uk

MICHEL MONTIGNAC

MONTIGNAC
RECIPES AND MENUS

Montignac Publishing U.K. Ltd.

First published in France under the title:
Recettes et menus Montignac

English version first published in 1994

Text © Nutrimont/Montignac Publishing UK Ltd.
Cover photo: G Larmuseau
Inside photos: KASPЯ Group.

ISBN 2 90 6236 62 4

Montignac Publishing UK Ltd
2 Mill Street
London W1R 9TE

www.montignac.publishing.com
info@montignac-publishing.com

ACKNOWLEDGEMENTS

This book could not have been written without the help of a number of experts, each of whom brought his or her own "savoir-faire" to the work.

So I am most grateful for the collaboration of:

Christiane CRABÉ, cordon bleu;
Claire GOFFART, dietician;
Françoise MATHEY, cordon-bleu;
Doctor Hervé ROBERT, specialist in nutrition;
Guy SANTORO, chef cuisinier, and his team at "Le Palmyre" restaurant in Cannes.

INTRODUCTION

Ever since the publication of *Dine out and lose weight* and *Eat yourself slim,* readers have been demanding a book of recipes and menus. For quite a while, I was reluctant to write such a book, because it did not really seem to me to be necessary. Or, what is worse, it even seemed a slightly dangerous thing to do. The method of eating which I recommend is not based on restrictions like a conventional diet, but on choice. It is a matter of changing our eating habits and adopting better ones. The result is that we can cut down excess weight (indeed, we can get rid of it completely), and at the same time guard against the risk of cardiovascular disease and enjoy increased vitality.

But to do this, we have to prepare the ground by making the effort to understand how our bodies work and by recognising three facts.

First, we have to realise that overweight is not so much a consequence of too rich a diet as the result of poor eating habits, which place too much reliance on processed foods and on foods deficient in nutrients.

Then we have to accept that traditional dietary advice, which recommends a hopelessly low calorie intake, is not only mistaken and ineffective, but is also dangerous; in the words of Dr. Hervé Robert, "It is undoubtedly the greatest scientific 'fudge' of the twentieth century".

And thirdly, we have to realise that what matters about food is its nutritional value in terms of fibre, trace elements and essential fatty acids. And it is precisely these nutrients, so vital to our survival, which have disappeared from the modern diet.

In addition, we need to understand the basic functioning of our metabolism and of our digestive tract.

And, finally, we have to learn to place foods in their correct category, and classify them in terms of the way they affect our metabolism.

Conventional dietary advice tends to produce mindless lists of complete menus, which may well lead to weight loss, but which simply reflect a mindless way of slimming, one that will inevitably prove disappointing and give only temporary results. What I am suggesting, on the other hand, certainly involves making choices in pursuit of the goal of a slim figure and a more vital state of health, but it also takes into account the availability of foods, what there happens to be on a restaurant menu, what you can buy in the shops or what you happen to have in the fridge.

In other words, if you have understood the principles underlying the dietary Method I am suggesting, there is no need for lists of specific menus or particular recipes. Whatever family, social or professional circumstances you find yourself in, you should be able to make appropriate choices and select what to eat accordingly.

I am always disconcerted when I meet people who tell me they have lost a great deal of weight by, as they quite incorrectly put it, "following the Montignac diet", and who have been astonished when they put it all back on again. These are invariably people who have applied some of the principles of the Method on a temporary basis and who have failed to understand that lasting results come not from depriving themselves of anything, but from adopting new eating habits permanently. Obviously, the same causes will produce the same effects each time, so as soon as they go back to a misguided way of eating, they inevitably suffer the same consequences as before.

This is why, quite early on, I gave up all attempts at summarising the Method or setting it out in "condensed" versions. Such versions, taken out of an explanatory and informative context, can only lead to fleetingly temporary results.

People who have not just tried to see the Method as some sort of slimming gimmick, but have made the effort to understand its full implications for their eating practices and philosophy, have not only obtained the lasting results they hoped for, but have at the same time discovered an inexhaustible source of health and well-being.

It is for them that *Montignac recipes and menus* has been written. In the full understanding of what they are doing, they will be able to explore further applications of a concept which they have already mastered.

A warning, therefore to others: if you have not yet had the chance to get acquainted with the basis of the Montignac Method, you may well be temped to over-simplify it by just following the suggestions in this volume. I cannot recommend to you too strongly that you first get to understand the principles underlying the Method by reading one of the previous books [1]. It really is the only way to gain the full benefit of this volume.

Even if you know how to choose the right foods and have completely understood the principles of the Method, it is not always easy to modify a traditional recipe so that it becomes a "Montignac recipe". This, however, is what we have tried to do in this book, with the help of a number of qualified professionals.

A further aim has been to provide the reader with nutritional information. Eating does not consist simply in satisfying our appetite or even our greed. The food we ingest must also provide all the nutrients our body needs to stay healthy.

Western society has recently become more aware of the fact that modern processed foods are lacking in many of these nutrients.

Hence the pharmaceutical industry urges us to consume food supplements in the form of tablets or capsules, a habit it finds much more lucrative than persuading us to change our eating habits.

---

(1) *Dine out and lose weight.* Artulen UK.
Eat yourself slim. Artulen UK.
Mettez un turbo dans votre assiette! Editions Artulen (available in French only).

But we should be aware that, quite apart from their considerable expense, these supplements are not well assimilated by our bodies when they are taken out of context. There seem to be substances present in natural foods which enable the body to make fullest use of the nutrients, even when present in only minute quantities.

The very fact of choosing the fibre-rich diet recommended by the Method and illustrated by the recipes in this book, automatically leads to consuming plenty of foods which are naturally rich in essential nutrients, such as vitamins, minerals and trace elements.

But, as well as selecting foods for their nutritive properties, it is also vital to know how to follow a few basic principles in storing and cooking them. At very least, we should know how to avoid the kinds of error which will lead to their essential nutrients being lost.

I cannot finish this introduction without reminding readers that we should never lose sight of the gastronomic quality of the dishes we prepare. Some may think that I do this only through my concern to preserve French cultural traditions, but it has been proved that such traditions and sound nutrition go hand in hand.

French culinary savoir-faire, which stems from regional country traditions, has always been the delight of gourmets, but it has also been the despair of conventional dieticians following the low-calorie school of thought. To those obsessed with calories, a love of good food, and the rich diet that implies, has been a thing to be frowned upon.

The most serious scientific studies carried out over recent years, though, have dealt a cutting blow to this view-point and have demonstrated that the exact opposite can be true.

It has now been shown that their traditional way of eating is one which has offered French people protection against the scourges of obesity and cardiovascular disease so prevalent in the United States and other western countries.

In both these respects France is the country which scores least badly, and the French way of eating is coming to be taken as a model.

A piece of good news which should encourage you to hurry off to the kitchen with renewed enthusiasm.

CHAPTER I

THE COMPOSITION AND
NUTRITIVE VALUE OF FOODS

Modern eating habits, largely imported from America, can be criticised on two grounds. First, the diet is dominated by processed foods, such as sugar and white flour, which are deficient in essential nutrients; by foods naturally devoid of such nutrients; and by those, such as potatoes, which lose most of their nutrients in cooking.

Secondly, there is so little variety in this food that the consumer always ends up eating the same things. The consequences show up in the form of deficiencies, or at very least relative deficiencies, of vitamins, minerals and trace elements.

In addition, the individual gradually loses the sense of taste and so misses out on the pleasures of the palate, which are one of the marks of the sophistication of our civilisation.

The way in which the food industry, supported by the chemical industry, is developing represents a real danger for the survival of our species; it is sounding the death-knell of evolution and opening the doors wide to our inevitable decline.

Science is now demonstrating, however, that the French culinary tradition embodies almost all the dietary virtues; as such, it is important that it should be preserved.

THE CLASSIFICATION OF FOODS

There is no point in repeating here the notions discussed in detail in other books. I should simply like to remind you of a few fundamental points.

Nutritionally, foods can be placed in one of two categories:

Energy-giving nutrients, whose functions are both to provide energy and to serve as the raw materials for a number of processes essential to the building or rebuilding of living matter. They are:

- Proteins
- Carbohydrates
- Lipids
- **Non-energy-giving nutrients,** needed for the energy-giving foods to be properly assimilated and metabolised and, in some cases, acting as catalysts to the various chemical reactions involved. They are:

- Fibre
- Water
- Vitamins
- Minerals
- Trace elements

Conventional dietary theory, whose rhetoric has evolved not one iota in thirty years, would have you believe that what counts is a balanced diet. According to this, each meal we eat should be made up of 15% protein, 55% carbohydrate and 30% fat.

We now know, however, that it is quite inadequate just to lay down such proportions, because when we say proteins, carbohydrates or fats, we need to know which ones we are talking about. Indeed, each of these three categories has sub-categories displaying widely differing characteristics.

As far as carbohydrates are concerned, they fall into two types:

Carbohydrates with a high glycaemic index (bad carbohydrates), which can have an adverse effect on our metabolism and lead indirectly to tiredness and weight gain.

Carbohydrates with a low glycaemic index (good carbohydrates), which have little or no undesirable effect on our metabolism and which are generally high in essential nutrients (vitamins, minerals and trace elements).

In the same way, it is both insufficient and dangerous to talk about lipids (fats) without being more specific. We now know that there are "good" lipids, that is those which lower cholesterol (fish, olive oil, goose fat) and "bad" lipids (butter and the fat of beef, lamb and pork), which lead to fats being deposited on the artery walls.

And as for proteins, we should take care to specify whether they are of animal or vegetable origin, because it is essential we eat some of each.

You can see, therefore, that it is senseless to talk about a balanced diet without taking account of the differences which exist within the major families of foods.

And yet that is precisely what old-fashioned dietary theory continues to do, knowing when it is "on to a good thing"; and the food industry has jumped on the bandwagon, with the media naively going along with it.

It is quite pitiful when you see even great French chefs making such appalling compromises as to use ready-prepared dishes whose nutritional content is highly suspect and complies with theories out of another age.

Before long, when the principles which we advocate of combining gastronomic pleasure with a healthy diet have definitively gained official recognition and swept away outdated prejudices, these people are going to look distinctly embarrassed and discredited.

We now know, too, that the role of non-energy-giving nutrients is critical, both for our metabolism to function correctly and for us to enjoy the best possible level of health and fitness.

So when we are shopping it is important to choose foods according to their nutritional content. The same concern should govern the storage and cooking of foods.

The following general information should help you to choose wisely.

RECOMMENDED DAILY INTAKE
OF MICRONUTRIENTS FOR A HEALTHY ADULT

– Potassium	3000 mg
– Calcium	800-1000 mg
– Phosphorus	800-1000 mg
– Magnesium	350 mg
– Sodium	4000 mg
– Iron	20 mg
– Copper	3 mg
– Zinc	15 mg
– Manganese	12 mg
– Fluoride	1 mg
– Provitamin A (Beta-carotene)	6 mg
– Vitamin A	1 mg
– Vitamin B1	1.5 mg
– Vitamin B2	1.8 mg
– Vitamin B5	10 mg
– Vitamin B6	2.2 mg
– Vitamin B9	400 µg
– Vitamin C	100 mg
– Vitamin D2	10 µg
– Vitamin E	15 mg
– Niacin	18 mg

NUTRITIONAL VALUE OF DIFFERENT FOODS

Some foods are richer than others in particular types of nutrients. The following list make help you to select appropriately:

Foods rich in beta-carotene (precursor of vitamin A)

Beta-carotene is an antioxidant which combats the free radicals associated with aging, cardiovascular disease and cancer.

- cress   - melon
- spinach   - apricots
- mango   - broccoli

In fact, all deeply coloured fruits and vegetables contain beta-carotene.

Foods rich in vitamin E

Vitamin E is an antioxidant which combats free radicals.

- wheatgerm   - oil-rich fruits and nuts
- all vegetable oils   - whole cereals
- margarine   - chocolate

Foods rich in folic acid (vitamin B9)

A deficiency of folic acid is dangerous in pregnant women and in elderly people.

- brewer's yeast   - green vegetables
- liver   - pulses
- oysters   - wholemeal bread
- soya

Foods rich in vitamin C (ascorbic acid)

Vitamin C is an antioxidant which combats free radicals and stimulates the immune system. Smokers tend to have low levels of vitamin C.

- blackcurrants   - lemons
- parsley   - broccoli
- kiwi   - fruit and vegetables
                             (especially eaten raw)

Care is needed as vitamin C is very unstable; it oxidises rapidly in air and is destroyed progressively in cooking.

TRACE ELEMENTS MINERALS	USES	SOURCES
Calcium	Needed for building the skeleton and teeth. A sufficient intake guards against osteoporosis.	cheese dairy products (even from skimmed milk) brewer's yeast sardines (with bones) eggs dried fruit, prunes "hard" water
Magnesium	Regulates muscle contraction. Settles the nervous system and counters the effects of stress.	winkles wheatgerm cocoa powder soya oil-rich fruits and nuts pulses wholemeal bread
Iron	Needed for an efficient immune system. Lack of it leads to anaemia, tiredness and infection. Iron of animal origin is much better absorbed in the gut than iron from vegetable sources.	black pudding (eaten once a week provides recommended weekly intake of iron) mussels red meats liver cocoa powder brewer's yeast
Zinc	Affects the absorption of carbohydrates through its action on insulin. Has antioxidant role and stimulates immune system.	oysters pulses duck liver brewer's yeast
Selenium	Antioxident which combats free radicals.	oysters chicken liver lobster pork and beef fish eggs mushrooms onions wholemeal bread

MINERALS AND TRACE ELEMENTS	USES	SOURCES
Chromium	Helps to metabolise carbohydrates and combats hyperinsulinism. An intake of it is vital to diabetics and overweight people.	egg yolk brewer's yeast fruit and vegetable skin cereal germs offal mushrooms oysters
Potassium	Affects the permeability of cells.	brewer's yeast dried apricots pulses prunes dates almonds, hazelnuts mushrooms bananas chocolate
Fluoride	Protects bones, ligaments and teeth.	tea mackerel sardines in oil St-Yorre water Vichy water Badoit water

ADVICE ON PRESERVING THE VITAMIN CONTENT OF FOODS

– Use the freshest ingredients you can get, rather than foods which have been on the shelves for days.

– If possible, buy your vegetables on a daily basis, in the market or from your local greengrocer.

– Use as little water as possible in preparation (washing, soaking).

– Choose to eat fruits and vegetables raw (except where this causes indigestion).

– Peel fruit and vegetables as little as possible and make only sparing use of the grater.

– Avoid long, slow cooking.

– Avoid keeping food warm for too long.

– Keep cooking water to use in soup; it contains water-soluble vitamins.

– Steam vegetables rather than boiling them.

– Organise your cooking so as not to have left-overs to refrigerate and heat up.

– Choose quality over quantity, buying organically grown items where possible.

– Roasting or grilling meat retains the most vitamins.

– Frozen foods have a higher vitamin content than tinned ones.

– Keep milk away from light.

COOKING, SAUCES AND SEASONINGS

Cooking:

– The use of fat is not essential; cook foods by steaming or braising, or in "parcels" or a court-bouillon, or by grilling if this is done well.

– Consider using non-stick pans, and avoid cooking on a horizontal spit.

– Outlaw chips.

– Avoid butter and banish palm oil.

– If you need to use fat, use olive oil, sunflower margarine or goose fat.

– Pressure-cooking is better than long, slow simmering.

– To the best of our present knowledge, microwave ovens are safe and nutrients are retained quite well. This does not mean it is a good idea to cook by microwave all the time.

Sauces:

– Some sauces make the dish too high in fat; it will then take longer to digest (4 to 5 hours).

– Simply deglaze the cooking residues from a dish (after draining off any fat), possibly adding a tablespoon of low-fat crème fraîche or some yogurt.

– To thicken a sauce without using flour, use a purée of cooked mushrooms made in the liquidiser; or add an egg yolk to a stew or casserole.

– You can add a knob of butter or a drizzle of olive oil to vegetables just before serving.

– From time to time you can enjoy a béarnaise sauce or some mayonnaise. But remember moderation is the watchword.

Seasonings:

– Make your own vinaigrette using oil, vinegar (or lemon) and mustard. Ready-made salad dressings are to be avoided, since they contain unwelcome additives, such as sugar and modified starches.

– You can make a fat-free salad dressing with lemon and "virtually fat-free" yogurt. But remember to keep consuming vegetable oils (olive or sunflower), to avoid a deficiency of essential fatty acids and vitamin E.

– Although a salt-free diet will do nothing to help you slim, that does not mean you should consume too much salt.

– Consider using garlic more; its numerous virtues include protecting against a number of diseases.

– Make sure your cooking is not insipid; enliven your dishes with spices and herbs.

FOODS WORTH CHOOSING REGULARLY

Garlic

Garlic is one of the oldest foods. It was consumed in the ancient world, where people seem to have realised intuitively how good it was for them. We know that the workers who built the Pyramids consumed garlic daily. Today its role has been reduced to that of a spice, and a much underestimated one considering its exceptional properties.

Garlic in fact contains various substances which have been shown to have a beneficial effect on our health. The allicin in it destroys harmful microscopic organisms and ensures the efficient formation of platelets, a key stage in blood coagulation.

The anticoagulant properties of garlic keep the blood thinner, so helping to prevent the thromboses which are often at the root of cardiovascular illness.

Other studies have shown that the consumption of garlic lowers the blood sugar level, the level of triglycerides and the level of LDL cholesterol. In addition, we know it brings blood pressure down, probably because of its diuretic properties.

Fish

Like meat, fish is an excellent source of protein but, unlike meat, it contains "good fats" which have a beneficial effect on our cardiovascular system.

In fact, fish oils bring down the level of triglycerides and contribute to raising the level of HDL cholesterol ("good cholesterol").

So it turns out, surprising though it may seem, that the oilier a fish is the higher the protection it offers against cardiovascular disease. We should therefore give a high profile to salmon, mackerel, herrings and sardines in our eating.

Yogurt

Some might think of yogurt as a modern food and, as such, associate it with the usual principles of factory production.

They would be mistaken, though, for its close cousin milk-curd has existed from time immemorial. They might also like to know that the first true yogurt officially appeared in France during the reign of François I. It was not until 1925 that the word found its way into the Larousse dictionary, and it was only after Bulgarian yogurt made its appearance in 1955 that it became really popular in France. But over the next thirty years, the French became second only to the Danes in yogurt consumption.

It is rather a pity that, although the gastronomic world has not exactly rejected yogurt, neither has it, in recent years, really taken it on board.

Its flavour, at least when it is properly made, merits closer attention. As for its nutritional qualities, they are such that yogurt ought to occupy a prominent place in any list of foods which "do us good".

One of the qualities of yogurt resides in its biological activity. It contains the active bacteria which form an essential part of our intestinal flora. In the course of digestion, these play their part in breaking down the foods we eat.

This essential collaboration between organisms is threatened in our modern diet, not only because this is not varied enough but also because we consume residual quantities of antibiotics in commercially produced meat or medicines.

A number of scientific studies have shown that yogurt not only boosts our consumption of calcium but also leads to a very marked improvement in cases of digestive or allergic problems.

Some studies have also noted increased production of interferon. This substance is fundamental to the functioning of the immune system, the body's defences against infection.

It had also been demonstrated that yogurt brings down cholesterol levels and may even have a role in preventing certain cancers.

So yogurt should be a part of a healthy eating programme. It even proves very useful in a number of cooked dishes (see recipe sections).

Olive oil

The "hands down" winner among the good fats, olive oil never ceases to amaze by the nutritional properties it displays.

It is extremely rich in monounsaturated fatty acids (oleic acid), and contains polyphenol and vitamins E and A, all of which go to make olive oil one of the most beneficial foods for our health.

Its many virtues are as follows:

– It lowers the overall cholesterol level and levels of triglycerides.
– It raises the level of "good" cholesterol (HDL).
– It produces improvement in cases of high blood pressure.
– It brings down the blood sugar level (an indirect factor in weight gain).
– It fights the free radicals implicated in aging and cancers.

This is why you are recommended to use olive oil–and not even in moderation. It should account for 25% to 50% of our fat intake.

In this connection, it has been noted that most of the Mediterranean countries, which have high consumption of olive oil, have particularly low incidence of cardiovascular disease.

Indeed, the region of the world where cardiovascular disease is the lowest and life expectancy the highest is Crete. Crete is the largest producer of olive oil in the world and its inhabitants are also the greatest consumers of it; olive oil represents 60% of their fat intake.

Brewer's yeast and wheatgerm

We know that modern foods which come off industrial production lines are lacking in essential nutrients (vitamins, minerals and trace elements).

This is why we need to be particularly vigilant in the way we choose foodstuffs, when we are shopping for the ingredients we use in our cooking.

But despite such precautions and even though we try our best to have a varied diet, we can never be certain we have the ideal intake of micronutrients.

We have already pointed out that synthetic food supplements, in the form of tablets and capsules, are poorly absorbed and therefore not effective enough to be worth their considerable expense.

However, there are two products which are whole foods in themselves and which are quite exceptional in terms of the essential nutrients they contain: these are dried brewer's yeast and wheatgerm. I encourage you strongly to consume them on a daily basis.

They are found in the guise of a variety of preparations, but it is worth seeking out the most natural and most economical forms available and avoiding products which contain additives and other undesirable preserving agents.

Brewer's yeast is also rich in chromium, which helps to improve glucose tolerance, thus leading to lower levels of sugar and insulin in the blood.

CONTENTSPER 100 G	DRIED BREWER'S YEAST	WHEATGERM
water	6 g	11 g
protein	42 g	26 g
carbohydrate	19 g	34 g
fats	2 g	10 g
fibre	22 g	17 g
potassium	1800 mg	850 mg
magnesium	230 mg	260 mg
phosphorus	1700 mg	1100 mg
calcium	100 mg	70 mg
iron	18 mg	9 mg
beta-carotene	0.01 mg	0 mg
vitamin B1	10 mg	2 mg
vitamin B2	5 mg	0.7 mg
vitamin B5	12 mg	1.7 mg
vitamin B6	4 mg	3 mg
vitamin B12	0.01 mg	0 mg
folic acid	4 mg	430 mg
niacin	46 mg	4.5 mg
vitamin E	0 mg	21 mg

CHAPTER II

FOODS WHOSE DIETARY VIRTUES
HAVE BEEN UNDERESTIMATED

There are some foods which have always appeared on the hit-list of conventional dieticians, whose ideas we know to be founded on belief rather than evidence. I refer in particular to wine, chocolate, foie gras and unpasteurised milk.

Scientific studies have now, thank Heaven, confirmed what was known intuitively even in antiquity. Indeed, not only is there nothing against consuming these products (in moderation), but we know that each in its own way has exceptional virtues in terms of nutrition.

The world of gastronomy has never been prepared to do without such items, which represent the fine flower of its traditions. And now the philosophy of combining gastronomic pleasure with a healthy diet not only demands that wine, chocolate, foie gras and unpasteurised milk resume their rightful position, but actually recommends them as foods with incomparable benefits for our health.

WINE

Dr. Maury[1] was quite right when he said: "Wine has allowed itself to be trapped in the ghetto of alcoholic drinks in general".

Legislation, abetted by a section of public opinion, has misguidedly lumped together all drinks containing alcohol. In reality, a very clear distinction should be drawn between natural ethyl

_____

(1) *La médecine par le vin,* Editions Artulen.

alcohol, which comes from fermenting fruit juice, and distilled alcohol, which is, in a sense, a synthetic product.

Wine is a food in itself, beneficial to health if consumed within the reasonable limit of half a litre per day, whereas it is in the nature of distilled alcohol to contain toxins.

1) Guarding against cardiovascular disease

A number of studies have shown that the countries where the most wine is drunk have a lower death toll from cardiovascular disease than other countries. The French, who drink ten times more wine than the Americans, have only a quarter the number of cardiovascular problems.

Even if other dietary factors also contribute to this, we now know that wine is positively beneficial in this respect. It has been demonstrated that fermented alcohol, consumed at up to a maximum of 30 g a day (the equivalent of half a bottle of Bordeaux), helps lower the overall blood cholesterol level and increases the proportion of "good cholesterol" (HDL cholesterol).

Quite apart from the beneficial effect of small quantities of alcohol, wine contains hundreds of other substances. Professor Masquelier has made a particular study of the polyphenols contained in the tannin; these are powerful antioxidants, which protect the artery walls and ward off the effects of aging. Wine also guards against thromboses because of the way it affects blood clotting.

2) Minerals and trace elements

Wine is indisputably one of the foods providing the highest concentration of minerals and trace elements. And we know that the modern diet is generally too low in these.

To be found in wine are copper, which protects against the development of mycosis; zinc, which is essential to sexual function; and magnesium and lithium, whose role in fighting stress is widely recognised. It also contains iron, to stimulate the immune system and prevent anaemia. And the calcium and manganese in it ensure that cells remain healthy.

Wine also contains soluble fibre, whose role has so far been insufficiently appreciated, but which plays a crucial role in regulating the digestion and absorption of carbohydrates and lipids (fats).

So it is apparent that, provided we consume it in only moderate quantities, wine is, as Pasteur said, *"the healthiest of drinks"*. Drinking it in moderation is unquestionably good for us.

CHOCOLATE

Chocolate, like wine, has proved itself nutritionally down through the centuries, but has unfairly had suspicion cast upon it by conventional dieticians.

It has been accused of every ill there is, not merely out of prejudice, but because the chocolate which has been on the market over recent years has been nothing more than sugar, lightly flavoured with cocoa. So the time has come to set matters straight on two counts: first by recognising that chocolate is exceptionally rich in nutrients, and secondly by making it clear that this applies only to bitter dark chocolate with a high (70%) cocoa content.

So it is not hard to see that what is good about chocolate is the cocoa and not all the substitutes or added substances it is loaded with for commercial reasons.

A good many scientific studies have shown that the accusations levelled against chocolate that it caused migraines, allergies, acne, digestive upsets, tooth decay, and so on, are again all part of the prejudice which has been handed down. Other studies have demonstrated the exceptional nutritive properties it has.

Cocoa butter, which makes up the fat content of chocolate, is composed mostly of monounsaturated fatty acids, the "good" fats, the ones which lower the "bad" cholesterol (LDL) level and help to raise the level of "good" cholesterol (HDL).

29

In addition, cocoa contains phytosterols, which bring down the level of triglycerides in the blood. And it has polyphenols, which have the property of protecting the artery walls.

This is what lead Professor Chaveron to declare that *"chocolate will soon have to be included in people's diet as part of the fight against the risk of cardiovascular disease"*.

As for the carbohydrates in chocolate, they have no unwanted effect on the blood sugar level, since the proteins and soluble fibre also present bring its glycaemic index down to 22. So it is true that *"chocolate does not necessarily make you fat"*.

We should also realise that chocolate is one of the best sources of magnesium, potassium, copper and vitamin E.

And finally, the presence of caffeine, theobromine and theophylline are responsible for chocolate's effect as a stimulant, and even as an aphrodisiac; while the phenylethylamine in it undoubtedly functions as an antidepressant.

All this explains why the consumption of dark chocolate containing at least 70% cocoa is greatly to be encouraged. Chocolate is not only a true gastronomic pleasure, but is also a food in itself with remarkable nutritive properties.

FOIE GRAS AND GOOSE FAT

Foie gras is undeniably symbolic of fine eating. For this reason it has always appeared suspect to conventional dieticians. The fact that it has a fat content of 45% could but persuade them to classify it among foods of doubtful dietary value, despite the qualities discernible to the palate. But over the last few years, a team of researchers has been demonstrating that foie gras can not only be absolved of any harmful effects, but constitutes a food amazingly rich in nutrients.

The pendulum began to swing in the mid-1980s, when a programme of studies sponsored by the World Health Organisation drew attention to the outstandingly good record of the French département of Gers. What could be the explanation of the fact that people living in this area had the highest life expectancy in France and that the incidence of cardiovascular disease was the lowest in the country? And indeed, France has in any case one of the best records in the world on these two points. Examining the statistics region by region showed that people living in South-West France did particularly well. But, even within that region, inhabitants of Gers were in a quite exceptional position, in that their life expectancy was 25% higher than that of people in neighbouring départments. So what could make the difference? The answer is simple, if surprising: it is the high consumption of goose and duck fat (including confits and foie gras) which changes the whole picture.

Doctor Renaud and his team at INSERM have demonstrated that, like olive oil, goose and duck fat contain a high proportion of oleic acid, which means they are foods which are particularly valuable in protecting the cardiovascular system.

As Doctor Renaud puts it, *"Nature has provided everything we need in order to enjoy good health"*. Not that we doubted that, but we are now discovering just how generous she has been to us.

UNPASTEURISED CHEESES

If Prince Charles had not rushed to the defence of cheeses made from unpasteurised milk at a time when they were at serious risk from European regulations, France might have lost one of its finest gastronomical prizes. The battle is not over yet, but the sanitised Brussels bureaucrats will now have an uphill task if they are to translate into reality their paranoid vision of hygiene and fermentation by chemicals.

But what French cheese producers may not realise is that if the finest cheese making establishments in the country were to be closed down, we should lose one of the most health-giving of foods.

Once again, conventional dietary theory has always cast opprobrium on cheese, claiming it contained too much fat and therefore too many calories. It was long believed that the fats in cheese were counterproductive in the fight to ward off cardiovascular disease.

But some did find it surprising that the French had four to six times less of this type of disease than other countries (notably the United States) where people either did not eat cheese or ate only an ersatz variety with the consistency of putty and the taste of soap. Wine consumption could not be the only explanation.

In the last few years, Doctor Renaud's research team has shown that the absorption of fat from fermented cheeses is actually much lower than had been thought. It seems that the fatty acids combine with the calcium in the insoluble salts and simply pass out of the body.

Other studies also show that the fermentation of raw milk, which is a natural process, leads to a complete change in the nature of the fats. The molecular structure of the saturated fat is altered in a way that limits its ability to be absorbed in the gut [2].

So traditional cheeses made from raw milk, unlike cheeses made from pasteurised milk, have no harmful effect on the cardiovascular system [3].

---

(2) Dietary fats (lipids) are 98% composed of triglycerides formed by one molecule of alcohol (glycerol) becoming attached to three molecules of fatty acid.

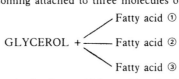

In saturated fats it is only the fatty acid in position 2 which is properly absorbed through the wall of the intestine. The fermentation of raw milk modifies the structure of the fats by largely suppressing fatty acids in position 2. And so, even though there is a great deal of saturated fat in a cheese made from unpasteurised milk, its absorption into the gut is reduced.

(3) Pasteurisation involves heating the milk to 72°C for 20 to 30 seconds. This has the effect of destroying the bacteria needed for fermentation and maturing. The milk then has to have bacteria artificially produced in specialised factories introduced into it.

So cheese made from pasteurised milk is an inert, industrially processed product, whose saturated fats remain unmodified. Cheese made from raw milk, on the other hand, is a living entity with real nutritional advantages.

There is even every reason to believe that natural fermentation, also found in yogurt, and maturing alter the chemical and physical characteristics of the milk in such a way that the consumption of unpasteurised cheeses may actually help in cutting down the risk of cardiovascular disease. It is a powerful argument which should point the European Commission in the right direction and one which the sanitising lobby will be unable to refute.

What is more, fermented milk products stimulate the heart muscle, help synthesise the B group vitamins, protect against various forms of pollution (such as those caused by the presence of nitrates), and may even prevent the occurrence of certain cancers.

The board laden with unpasteurised cheeses, which has unfortunately tended to disappear even from menus with gourmet pretensions, should be rehabilitated forthwith.

As we have seen, there is no lack of convincing arguments. To which we could always add the comment of Maupassant, who made the charming observation that *"a meal without cheese was as dull as a kiss without a moustache"*.

It was the Americans who first brought in large-scale pasteurisation, forbidding the use of raw milk because of fears of food poisoning.

Statistics show, however, that in the rare cases of contamination that have occurred the cheeses implicated have invariably been made from pasteurised milk. Moreover, experience shows that the longer the a cheese has matured the lower are the risks.

CHAPTER III

PHASE I MENUS
FOR THREE MONTHS

As I pointed out in the introduction to this volume, I was very reluctant to suggest a list of menus. Again, this is because I consider that anyone who has understood the basis of the Method should be able to work out menus which comply with it.

However, I would concede that sometimes the imagination needs prompting, so that a list can be very helpful in providing ideas.

A word of warning, though, to anyone who might suppose you could apply the Method effectively for the first time just from this book. It would be rather like thinking you could drive a car in a city like Paris after learning to drive in the desert.

The menus set out in this chapter all correspond to the demands of Phase I. If you have thoroughly understood the Method, you will realise there is no point in having menus for Phase II, because what makes Phase II different from Phase I is that discrepancies are allowed.

The menus give examples of mid–day and evening meals. No details of breakfasts have been given, because the thinking behind breakfast is always more or less the same.

Breakfast should take the form of a complete meal and it is important not to neglect it. So we thought it might be useful to remind you here of the underlying principles. In the table of menus which follows dishes are marked * where the recipe is given in the relevant recipe section.

BREAKFAST

A) On waking

Eat some fruit if you like; indeed, you are strongly advised to do so. You can add fresh fruit juice such as lemon, orange or grapefruit (without sugar), squeezed at the last moment to avoid losing all the vitamins. Bottled fruit juices, even if they are 100 % natural, are of no nutritional interest.

Then go on with your morning routine, waiting at least twenty minutes before returning to your breakfast proper.

B) Choice of foods

* **Formula No 1:** breakfast of protein and carbohydrate + fibre

Bread option:
– bread rich in fibre (wholemeal or with bran)
– Scandinavian 'wasa' crispbread
Accompanied by:
– fruit spread containing no sugar
– 'very low fat' fromage frais or 'very low fat' yogurt.

Cereal option:
– whole cereals without sugar (but not corn flakes)
– muesli without sugar
– oat flakes
With hot or cold skimmed milk.
– 'very low fat' fromage frais or
– 'very low fat' yogurt.

* **Formula No 2:** fruit only

You can breakfast solely on fruit.

This option gives you good carbohydrates, fibre, minerals and vitamins. It has no protein though; so the ideal would be to add at least one skimmed milk product.

It does not have any cereal content, either, and this is an element you may not have occasion to include later in the day.

* **Formula No 3:** savoury, or protein and lipid breakfast

This will be composed of ham, bacon, eggs and cheese and will be eaten without bread.

Unfortunately, it gives you no carbohydrates or fibre, and it is high in saturated fats, which is likely to raise your cholesterol level if you are predisposed to this problem.

This type of breakfast, therefore, is to be avoided by anyone with a cardiovascular problem or with diabetes. It should, in any case, be eaten only occasionally (if, for example, you are staying in a hotel).

To drink:

- coffee, preferably decaffeinated
- tea
- skimmed milk
- chicory
- soya milk
- avoid chocolate in Phase I.

SNACKS AND AFTERNOON TEA

If your breakfast and two main meals have been well thought out, there should be no reason suddenly to feel peckish at other times; you should be able to wait for the next meal, without having to eat anything in between.

So there is no justification for adults to have 'elevenses' or afternoon tea, unless they are taking part in an endurance sport. If you have to make an exception to the rule, you are advised to eat a piece of fresh fruit, preferably an apple.

And in any case, never confuse 'having tea' with 'having a nibble'

THE EVENING MEAL

This should be the lightest meal of the day but, unfortunately, for social reasons, it is often the heaviest.

Those aspiring to lose weight should take note that it is fats consumed in the evening that are the most readily laid down as body fat. Our biological clock decrees that the process of absorption is most active during the night. It has been shown that the same quantity of fat (of whatever type) consumed through the first half of the day has less chance of being absorbed and being transformed into reserves of body fat.

It is worth noting, too, that proteins and lipids require a longer period for digestion and this may interfere with the quality of our sleep, so that we feel less refreshed afterwards.

This is why I would advise making meals at home which are protein and carbohydrate with fibre, using any of the following foods:

Starter:

  - vegetable soup (avoiding potatoes and carrots)
  - various salads dressed with 'very low fat' yogurt and lemon
  - artichokes or green vegetables

Main dish:

  - brown rice (with tomato coulis)
  - wholewheat pasta (with tomato and basil coulis)
  - lentils with onions
  - haricot or red kidney beans
  - whole semolina couscous with vegetables (no meat)

38

– variety of vegetables, such as cauliflower or leeks

To complete the meal:

– fruit mousse (see bavarois recipes)
– 'summer' fruits, such as strawberries, raspberries or blackberries (but not cherries)
– a low fat fromage frais or yogurt

DESSERTS

In Phase I, an occasional discrepancy in the form of something other than cheese can be allowed, for example, on Sunday. If you do this, you will have to choose a dessert from those marked 'very slight discrepancy' (see Page 249).

MENU SUGGESTIONS

FIRST MONTH – Week 1

		MONDAY	TUESDAY	WEDNESDAY	THURSDAY	FRIDAY	SATURDAY	SUNDAY
LUNCH		Red cabbage	Mackerel in white wine	Cucumber with yogurt and mint*	Asparagus in vinaigrette	Eggs mimosa*	Salad of mussels*	Beansprouts salad with scampi*
		Tuna omelette*	Turkey escalope	Roast beef	Hake gratiné	Roast chicken	Lamb chops with mint*	Red mullet with Provençal vegetables*
		–	Brussels sprouts	Provençal vegetable mould*	Courgettes	Braised chicory	Salsify	–
		Green salad	Green salad	–	–	–	Green salad	–
		Cheese	Yogurt	Cheese	Cheese	Cheese	Cheese	Summer fruits mousse*
DINNER		Radishes with salt	Tomato salad	Cream of mushroom soup	Vegetable soup	Aubergine caviar*	Artichokes with Roquefort*	Cream of broccoli soup*
		Wholewheat tagliatelle (mushroom and very low fat fromage frais sauce)	Raw cured ham	Haricot beans (very low fat fromage frais and parsley sauce)	Grilled salmon Spinach (with low fat cream)	Stuffed onions	Grilled tuna with bacon* French beans	Lentils with onions
		–	Turnips with parsley	–	–	–	–	–
		Low fat yogurt•	Fromage frais	Low fat yogurt•	Fromage frais	Yogurt	Fromage frais	Low fat yogurt•

Note: * denotes recipe given in this book

• May be flavoured with fruit preserve without added sugar

FIRST MONTH – Week 2

		MONDAY	TUESDAY	WEDNESDAY	THURSDAY	FRIDAY	SATURDAY	SUNDAY
LUNCH		Tomato salad	Palm hearts	Sardines in olive oil	Leeks with vinaigrette	Chicory salad	Greek salad*	Baked eggs with mixed salad*
		Rabbit with parsley	Fillet of cod with lemon	Entrecôte	Sautéed turkey*	Fillet of hake	Squid with tomato and onions	Grilled fillet steak
		Braised celeriac	Cauliflower	French beans	Spinach (with low fat cream)	Cabbage	–	Artichoke bases with mushrooms*
		–	–	–	–	–	Green salad	–
		Cheese	Cheese	Cheese	Cheese	Cheese	Cheese	Raspberry bavarois*
DINNER		Mussel soup*	–	Vegetable broth	Clear vegetable soup	–	Cucumber with yogurt and mint*	Green salad with saucisson*
		Rock salmon	Brown rice and aubergine bake*	Chicken breast	Haricot beans (very low fat fromage frais sauce)	Cheese omelette	Provençal vegetable mould*	Courgettes with fromage frais stuffing*
		Fried mushrooms	Turnips with parsley	Green salad	–	Frisée lettuce with lardons	–	–
		Yogurt	Low fat yogurt•	Fromage frais	Low fat yogurt•	Fromage frais	Fromage frais with sultanas	Yogurt

• May be flavoured with fruit preserve without added sugar.

FIRST MONTH – Week 3

	MONDAY	TUESDAY	WEDNESDAY	THURSDAY	FRIDAY	SATURDAY	SUNDAY
LUNCH	Radishes with butter Piperade* Broccoli – Cheese	Crab, avocado and artichoke salad* Pork chops with herbs Salsify – Cheese	Cauliflower in vinaigrette Grilled minced steak Peas with onion – Cheese	Artichokes in vinaigrette Poached mackerel with leeks in cream sauce* – – Cheese	Tomato salad Sliced heart Spinach purée Green salad Cheese	Seafood salad* Veal chops with French bean and cheese topping* – Green salad Cheese	Salad of goose gizzards Scallops on a bed of leeks* – – Grand Marnier mousse*
DINNER	Savoury fromage frais mould* Split pea purée* – Low fat yogurt*	Beansprout salad Boiled eggs Green salad Cheese	Sorrel soup Lentils with tomato* – Low fat yogurt*	Vegetable soup Chicken breast Braised chicory Fromage frais	Salad of mixed summer vegetables Aubergines stuffed with mushroom purée and fromage frais – Yogurt	Celery salad Parcels of salmon steak with sorrel and mint – Fromage frais	Cream of radish soup* Wholemeal spaghetti with courgettes and mint – Very low fat* fromage frais

* May be flavoured with fruit preserve without added sugar.

FIRST MONTH – week 4

	MONDAY	TUESDAY	WEDNESDAY	THURSDAY	FRIDAY	SATURDAY	SUNDAY
LUNCH	Celeriac with rémoulade dressing	Mixed cabbage salad	Tomatoes stuffed with tuna*	Chicory salad	Dandelion salad with lardons	Magret de canard with leek and raspberries*	Eggs mimosa*
	Grilled poussin	Skate with capers	Grilled black pudding	Roast pork	Steak au poivre	Sautéed prawns with ratatouille*	Shoulder of lamb in lemon*
	Peas and turnips	Purée of French beans	Cauliflower purée	Aubergine gratin	French beans	–	Lettuce and sorrel mousseline*
	–		Green salad				
	Cheese	Cheese	Cheese	Cheese	Yogurt	Cheese	Chocolate soufflé*
DINNER	Vegetable soup	Vegetable bouillon	Palm hearts	Pumpkin soup	Cream of asparagus soup	Cucumber (very low fat fromage frais dressing)	Salad of mussels*
	Fillet of whiting	Split pea purée*	Courgettes with fromage frais stuffing*	Curried brown and wild rice	Eggs baked in tomato*	Broad beans with with artichokes*	Leek soufflé*
	–	–	–		Green salad	–	–
	Yogurt	Very low fat* fromage frais	Yogurt	Very low fat* fromage frais	Cheese	Very low fat* fromage frais	Cheese

*May be flavoured with fruit preserve without added sugar.

SECOND MONTH – week 1

		MONDAY	TUESDAY	WEDNESDAY	THURSDAY	FRIDAY	SATURDAY	SUNDAY
LUNCH		Lamb's lettuce	Tomato salad	White cabbage with lardons*	Cucumber salad	Smoked trout fillet	Salmon in white fish	Beansprout salad with scampi*
		Escalope of turkey	Turbot moulds with watercress coulis*	Grilled chicken	Rabbit with bacon and cabbage*	Magret of duck	Ox tongue gratin*	Sole with prawn and mushroom*
		Braised courgettes	Cauliflower	Salsify	–	Celeriac sautéed in goose fat*	Braised aubergines	Mushrooms with parsley
		Cheese	Cheese	Cheese	Cheese	Cheese	Cheese	'Floating islands'*
DINNER		Cream of mushroom soup	Vegetable bouillon	Vegetable soup	Artichoke hearts	French beans (with a drizzle of lemon)	Smoked ham	Cream of watercress soup
		Haricot beans (very low fat fromage frais dressing)	Gratin of ham and asparagus (with low fat cream, not white sauce)	Lentils with onion	Soft-boiled eggs	Wholemeal spaghetti with courgettes*	Baked tomatoes with parsley	Wholemeal semolina with vegetables (no meat or fat)
		–		–	Spinach purée	–	Green salad	–
		Low fat yogurt*	Fromage frais	Low fat yogurt*	Fromage frais	Low fat yogurt*	Yogurt	Very low fat* fromage frais

* May be flavoured with fruit preserve without added sugar.

SECOND MONTH – week 2

	MONDAY	TUESDAY	WEDNESDAY	THURSDAY	FRIDAY	SATURDAY	SUNDAY
LUNCH	Chicory salad	Salad of mixed summer vegetables*	Seafood salad*	Celeriac with rémoulade dressing	French beans	Eggs in aspic*	Green salad with foie gras*
	Leg of lamb	Grilled tuna with bacon*	Steak tartare	Pork chop	Grilled kidneys	Parcels of salmon fillets with purée of green peppers*	Spiced veal with artichokes*
	French beans with parsley –	Purée of celeriac Green salad	– Green salad	Spinach purée –	Cauliflower –	– –	– Green salad
	Cheese	Cheese	Cheese	Cheese	Cheese	Cheese	Raspberry bavarois*
DINNER	Tomato soup	Vegetable soup	Palm hearts	Mussel soup*	Vegetable bouillon	Vegetable bouillon	Cream of tomato soup
	Fried eggs	Broad beans with artichokes*	Fish soufflé*	Tomatoes with mushroom stuffing*	Raw cured ham	Wholemeal tagliatelle with mushroom purée	Courgettes with very low fat fromage frais stuffing*
	Braised lettuce	–	Broccoli with slivered almonds*	–	Braised chicory	–	–
	Yogurt	Very low fat• fromage frais	Yogurt	Fromage frais	Yogurt	Very low fat• fromage frais	Low fat• yogurt

• May be flavoured with fruit preserve without added sugar.

SECOND MONTH – Week 3

		MONDAY	TUESDAY	WEDNESDAY	THURSDAY	FRIDAY	SATURDAY	SUNDAY
LUNCH		–	Salad of 'ocean sticks'	Beansprout salad	Mushrooms à la grecque	Oriental salad*	Fish loaf*	Eggs mimosa*
		Baked eggs with anchovy*	Roast chicken	Lamb's heart kebabs*	Sole with prawns and mushroom*	Sautéed turkey*	Duck breasts in green pepper sauce*	Roast beef
		Spinach gratin	Salsify	Fennel gratin	Purée of French beans	Purée of pumpkin	Leek soufflé*	Braised lettuce
		Green salad	Green salad	–	–	Green salad	Green salad	–
		Cheese	Cheese	Cheese	Cheese	Cheese	Cheese	Baked summer fruits dessert*
DINNER		–	White cabbage with lardons*	Cream of mushroom soup	–	Mushroom and garlic fromage frais mould*	–	Chilled cucumber soup*
		Parcel of cod fillet	Chicory and ham (with low fat cream and eggs, not béchamel)	Brown rice and aubergine bake*	Pot-au-feu*	Celeriac and Parmesan fritters*	Smoked haddock with yogurt sauce*	Chickpeas in tomato
		Purée of watercress	–	–	Leeks, turnips, cabbage	–	Courgette gratin	–
		Yogurt	Fromage frais	Low fat yogurt*	Fromage frais	Yogurt	Fromage frais	Low fat yogurt*

* May be flavoured with fruit preserve without added sugar.

SECOND MONTH – Week 4

		MONDAY	TUESDAY	WEDNESDAY	THURSDAY	FRIDAY	SATURDAY	SUNDAY
LUNCH		Cauliflower vinaigrette	Salad with paprika dressing*	Sardines with salad*	Cucumber salad	Leeks vinaigrette	Asparagus bavarois*	Mousse of Parma ham with leeks*
		Marinated beef*	Fillets of sole with aubergine purée	Entrecôte with Roquefort	Roast pork	Escalope of turkey	Curried mussel stew*	Ballotins of hare*
		Asparagus		Brussels sprouts	Braised celeriac	French beans	Spinach salad	Peas with turnip / Green salad
		–	Green salad		–	–		Mango bavarois with a kiwi coulis*
		Cheese	Cheese	Cheese	Cheese	Cheese	Cheese	
DINNER		Sorrel soup	Tomato salad (with drizzle of lemon)	Cucumber salad	Radishes	Eggs in aspic*	Vegetable soup	Goat's cheese soufflé*
		Mushroom omelette	Wholemeal semolina with vegetables	Chicken breast / Braised chicory	Red kidney beans with onion (mushroom and very low fat fromage frais sauce)	Parcel of cod fillet	Split pea purée*	Stuffed cabbage
		Green salad			Green salad	Green salad		
		–	–	–	–		–	–
		Cheese	Low fat yogurt•	Fromage frais	Low fat yogurt•	Fromage frais	Low fat yogurt•	Fromage frais

• May be flavoured with fruit preserve without added sugar.

THIRD MONTH – Week 1

LUNCH

	MONDAY	TUESDAY	WEDNESDAY	THURSDAY	FRIDAY	SATURDAY	SUNDAY
	Artichokes with fromage frais and Roquefort*	Mackerel in white wine	Cucumber salad	Radishes with butter	Eggs in aspic*	Baked spinach and clams*	Goat's cheese soufflé*
	Rabbit with Mediterranean vegetables*	Lamb chops	Pork fillet	Red mullet with Provençal vegetables*	Fillet steak with mushrooms*	Poussins in lime sauce*	Basque-style chicken*
	–	Braised chicory or lettuce	Gratin of salsify	–	–	Lettuce and sorrel mousseline*	–
	Cheese	Green salad Cheese	– Cheese	Green salad Cheese	Green salad Cheese	Cheese	Strawberries and whipped cream Nata*

DINNER

	MONDAY	TUESDAY	WEDNESDAY	THURSDAY	FRIDAY	SATURDAY	SUNDAY
	Vegetable bouillon	Lamb's lettuce and tomato salad	Vegetable soup	Cream of cauliflower soup	Crudités (with a drizzle of lemon)	–	Cream of broccoli soup*
	Wholemeal semolina with vegetables	Leeks and ham (with low fat cream and eggs, not béchamel)	Pumpkin gratin (with fromage frais sauce)	Fish soufflé with watercress sauce*	Lentils with onion	Sole coated with Parmesan* French beans	Tuna omelette*
	–	–	–	Green salad	–	Green salad	Frisée
	Low fat• fromage frais	Fromage frais	Yogurt	Fromage frais	Low fat yogurt•	Fromage frais	Yogurt

• May be flavoured with fruit preserve without added sugar.

	MONDAY	TUESDAY	WEDNESDAY	THURSDAY	FRIDAY	SATURDAY	SUNDAY
LUNCH	Palm hearts	Salad of mixed summer vegetables*	White cabbage with lardons*	Tuna in aspic*	Beansprout salad	Foie gras with green salad*	Salmon trout terrine with fennel*
	Veal escalope	Cod with tomato coulis	Grilled black pudding	Ham omelette	Duck breasts in green pepper sauce*	Shoulder of lamb in lemon*	Provençal beef casserole*
	Celery	Braised lettuce	French beans	–	Peas with onion	Broccoli	Aubergines
	–	Green salad	–	Green salad	–	–	–
	Cheese	Cheese	Cheese	Cheese	Cheese	Cheese	Rhubarb bavarois with raspberry coulis*
DINNER	Gaspacho*	Watercress soup	Vegetable soup	Leek soup	Cucumber with yogurt and mint*	Cream of asparagus soup	Leek soufflé*
	Broad beans with artichokes*	Chicken liver ramekins*	Fillet of hake	Tomatoes with mushroom stuffing*	Wholemeal spaghetti with courgettes*	Eggs baked in tomato*	Green salad
	Low fat yogurt•	Fromage frais	Yogurt	Fromage frais	Low fat yogurt•	Fromage frais	Fromage frais

* May be flavoured with fruit preserve without added sugar.

THIRD MONTH – Week 3

		MONDAY	TUESDAY	WEDNESDAY	THURSDAY	FRIDAY	SATURDAY	SUNDAY
LUNCH		Mixed cabbage salad	Crab, avocado and artichoke salad*	Mackerel in white wine	Eggs mimosa*	Poultry terrine*	White fish and watercress terrine*	Salmon and spinach terrine*
		Roast chicken	Rabbit with green olives*	Basque-style pot-roast veal*	Parcels of whiting fillets	Trout with melted cheese topping*	Casseroled chicken	Sole coated in Parmesan*
		Celery 'chips'	Turnips	Courgettes	Aubergine purée	Braised fennel	–	Broccoli
		–	Green salad	–	–	Green salad	Green salad	–
		Cheese	Cheese	Cheese	Cheese	Cheese	Cheese	Chocolate and vanilla bavarois*
DINNER		–	French beans	Cucumber with low fat yogurt dressing	Vegetable soup	Cream of leek soup	Dandelion salad with lardons	Mussel soup*
		Wholewheat spaghetti (with tomato and basil coulis)	Asparagus and ham gratin (with low fat cream and eggs, not béchamel)	Split pea purée*	Cold roast pork	Artichoke bases with mushrooms*	Ballotins of fish with cabbage*	Chicory with anchovies
		–	–	–	Green salad	–	–	Green salad
		Low fat yogurt•	Fromage frais	Very low fat• fromage frais	Fromage frais	Fromage frais	Yogurt	Cheese

• May be flavoured with fruit preserve without added sugar.

THIRD MONTH – Week 4

	MONDAY	TUESDAY	WEDNESDAY	THURSDAY	FRIDAY	SATURDAY	SUNDAY
LUNCH	Mushroom salad	Curried hard-boiled eggs	Tomatoes stuffed with tuna*	Cucumber salad	Red cabbage vinaigrette	Mousse of parma ham and leeks*	Asparagus bavarois*
	Grilled minced steak	Baked coley	Parcels of calf's liver*	Beef, pork and veal goulasch*	Roast veal	Grilled sardines	Roast mallard with purée of cep mushrooms*
	French beans with parsley	Courgettes	Lettuce and sorrel mousseline*	Turnip purée	Broccoli	Celery purée	–
	–	Green salad	–	Green salad	–	–	Apricot mousse*
	Cheese	Cheese	Cheese	Cheese	Cheese	Cheese	Cheese
DINNER	Onion soup	Vegetable soup	Cauliflower salad	Vegetable bouillon	Fish soup	–	Cream of watercress soup
	Minced beef in a cheese soufflé*	Split-pea gratin with tomato and onions	Chicken breast	Artichokes and asparagus with cheese topping*	Tomatoes with mushroom stuffing*	Brown rice and aubergine bake*	Skate with salad*
	Green salad	–	Peppers baked in olive oil	Frisée lettuce with lardons	–	Green salad (with a drizzle of lemon)	–
	Yogurt	Very low fat* fromage frais	Yogurt	Fromage frais	Cheese	Very low fat* fromage frais	Cheese

* May be flavoured with fruit preserve without added sugar.

SEASONAL PRODUCE

	FISH SHELLFISH	MEAT FOWL	VEGETABLES	FRUITS
Spring (March, April, May)	shad gilt-head gudgeon coley dab ray red mullet trout lobster crab mackerel	lamb veal guineafowl	salsify asparagus spinach sorrel cress web lettuce cos lettuce peas lettuce	rhubarb strawberry lemon
Summer (June, July, August)	eel bass gilt-head gudgeon herring perch plaice sole tuna mackerel shrimp lobster crayfish sardine	guineafowl veal rabbit hen chicken duck pigeon	lettuce artichoke beet cucumber gherkin green beans tomato egg-plant marrow	apricot gooseberry raspberry strawberry fig cherry plum grapefruit peach whortleberry
Autumn (September, October, November)	carp mussels fresh cod	venison partridge boar pigeon pork mutton hare	cardoon root celery branch celery cabbage cauliflower red cabbage kidney beans turnip pumpkin	blackcurrant lemon fig pear apple plum grapes hazelnut chestnut banana nuts

	FISH SHELLFISH	MEAT FOWL	VEGETABLES	FRUITS
Winter (December, January, February)	fresh cod carp herring coley dab whiting cod salmon sole turbot oysters mussels fish roe	beef mutton pork pheasant cock turkey hen	broccoli brussels sprouts chicory lambs lettuce dandelion	pineapple banana chestnut quince mandarin nuts orange grapefruit apple

PHASE I RECIPES

If you are following the dietary principles of the Montignac Method, Phase I is the period during which the ground rules are laid down. These rules form the basis of the new approach to eating which you have decided to embark upon and to pursue.

The purpose of Phase I is better to enable you to attain the objectives which you have set yourself and which, of course, you aim to make permanent:

– Weight loss;
– Protection against cardiovascular disease;
– Increased physical and intellectual vitality;
– Doing away with any gastric and digestive problems;
– Doing away with sudden bouts of tiredness and other forms of fatigue;
– Better sleep.

I cannot emphasize too heavily that merely following the recipes set out here cannot in any circumstances lead to long-term results; the basic principles of the Method have first to be understood and accepted.

Though, of course, anyone can gain inspiration from these recipes simply in order to enjoy the dishes, to discover how to make them and to benefit from their good nutritional content.

Some people may believe that there can be no possible place for any dessert in Phase I. However, at the risk of shocking the purists, we have tried hard to think up a few. After all, there are times in family life when a dessert is called for. At such times you simply have to choose from among the desserts which present only a "very slight discrepancy". The discrepancy involved is indeed so slight that there is no justification for excluding them entirely. However, properly pursuing Phase I does not allow you to include them at every meal. By integrating them into your plan once a week, on Sunday maybe, as suggested in the menu section, you can enjoy them without running any risks.

STARTERS

Cream of radish soup
Crème de radis

Serves 4

Preparation: 10 minutes
Cooking time: 10 minutes

Ingredients:

2 bunches radishes with leaves
2 leeks
100 ml low-fat crème fraîche
1 litre chicken stock
Salt, pepper
2 tablespoons olive oil

Wash the radishes, complete with their leaves, and the leeks. Chop both finely and fry gently in the olive oil.

Bring the stock up to the boil and add to the vegetables. Cook on a high heat for 5 minutes. Blend to a purée and sieve.

Season with salt and pepper. Reheat the soup before serving and add the crème fraîche at the last minute.

Cream of broccoli soup
Velouté de brocolis

Serves 4

Preparation: 15 minutes
Cooking time: 30 minutes

Ingredients:

500 g broccoli
100 g vegetables
(leeks, celery sticks)
1/4 litre low-fat crème fraîche
1/4 litre chicken stock
2 tablespoons olive oil
3 tablespoons fines herbes
3 shallots, thinly sliced
Salt, pepper

Wash the broccoli and remove the florets from the stalk. Trim and peel the stalks as necessary and cut into pieces.

Wash and dice the leeks and celery sticks. Soften in the olive oil over a gentle heat. Add the sliced shallots.

Add the broccoli, the fines herbes and the stock. Bring to the boil and simmer until all the vegetables are cooked (about 25 minutes).

Put the soup through a blender, adding the crème fraîche. Return to a low heat for 5 minutes and season with salt and pepper.

Serve hot.

Chilled cucumber soup
Potage glacé aux concombres

Serves 4

Preparation: 15 minutes
Refrigeration: 1 hour

Ingredients:

2 cucumbers
4-6 tablespoons single cream
1/2 clove garlic
2 shallots
1 tablespoon tarragon vinegar
A few sprigs dill
Salt, pepper

Peel the cucumbers and cut them lengthways. Remove the seeds, cover with rough salt to draw out the liquid and put to one side.

Peel the garlic and shallots. Dry the cucumber with absorbent kitchen paper and blend with the garlic, shallots, vinegar and cream, to make a very smooth soup.

Season with salt and pepper and place in the refrigerator for one hour. Serve garnished with a few sprigs of dill.

Mussel soup
Soupe aux moules

Serves 4

Preparation: 20 minutes
Cooking time: 15 minutes

Ingredients:

1 litre mussels
4 tablespoons olive oil
100 ml white wine
100 g low-fat crème fraîche
1 egg yolk
1 finely sliced onion
1/2 clove garlic
Dash of lemon juice
1 tablespoon chopped parsley
Salt, pepper, curry powder

Clean the mussels, rinsing them several times. Fry the onion gently in the olive oil until it turns pale golden, and then pour the white wine over.

Add a glass of water and place the mussels in the liquid over a high heat to open them up. Remove and shell the mussels. Strain the liquid and return it to the pan.

Bring the liquid back to the boil. Then add the lemon juice, the salt and pepper, a pinch of curry powder, the parsley and the garlic. Simmer gently for 8 minutes.

Whisk the egg yolk and crème fraîche together and stir into the soup. Finally, add the shelled mussels. Serve hot.

Mushroom and garlic fromage frais mould. p.70.

Beef Carpaccio. p.134

Quails' eggs with scallops. p.225

Cream of btoccoli soup. p.62

Cucumber sorbet served with a tomato coulis. p.77.

Chilled Spanish summer vegetable soup
Gaspacho

Serves 6

Preparation: 30 minutes
Refrigeration: 3 hours

Ingredients:

1 kg tomatoes
1 cucumber
1 red and 1 green pepper
1 fresh fennel bulb (raw)
1 stick celery
3 onions
3 cloves garlic
3 tablespoons olive oil
2 tablespoons vinegar
1/2 litre water or vegetable
stock (degreased)
1 tray ice-cubes
Salt, pepper

Plunge the tomatoes into boiling water for 30 seconds, skin and remove the seeds. Peel the cucumber. Put aside a few slices of cucumber and one onion; dice these finely and keep for decoration.

Cut up all the vegetables and put them through the blender. Add the water or vegetable stock, olive oil and vinegar.

Season with salt and pepper and leave in the refrigerator for three hours for the flavours to develop.

Immediately before serving, stir in the ice cubes and sprinkle the soup with the little pieces of cucumber and onion.

Savoury fromage frais mould
Flan au fromage blanc

Serves 4

Preparation: 15 minutes
Cooking time: 40 minutes

Ingredients:

200 g fromage frais
100 ml low-fat crème fraîche
50 g black olives, pitted
4 eggs
2 tomatoes
30 g butter
1 pinch oregano, salt, pepper

Plunge the tomatoes into boiling water for 30 seconds, skin and remove the pips. Chop and cover with rough salt; leave for about 30 minutes to draw off the juice, then drain.

Mix the fromage frais with the crème fraîche. Add the eggs, lightly beaten. Season with salt, pepper and the oregano.

Add the pieces of olive and the tomatoes, mix the ingredients thoroughly and pour the mixture into a buttered charlotte mould. Cook in a gentle oven (150° C, 300°F, gas mark 2) for 40 minutes.

This dish can be served tepid or cold with, for example, a tomato coulis (see page 77).

Goat's cheese soufflé
Soufflé au fromage de chèvre

Serves 6

Preparation: 15 minutes
Cooking time: 20 minutes

Ingredients:

200 g fromage frais
50 g fresh goat cheese
4 eggs, separated
Olive oil (for the ramekins)
Salt, pepper

Blend the fromage frais with the goat cheese. Add the egg yolks, salt and pepper.

Beat the egg whites until they form stiff peaks and fold them gently into the cheese mixture, a little at a time. Oil six ramekins and divide the mixture between them.

Make a bain-marie by placing 2 cm of boiling water in a large dish. Stand the ramekins in the water.

Place in the centre of the oven, preheated to 200°C (400°F, gas mark 6), for 15 to 20 minutes. Serve the soufflés immediately they are cooked.

Ham mousse served with a tomato coulis
Mousse de jambon et son coulis de tomates

Serves 4

Preparation: 25 minutes
Refrigeration: 12 hours

Ingredients:

320 g mild cooked ham
300 g fromage frais
4 egg whites
1 1/2 leaves (or 1/2 sachet) gelatine
20 ml madeira or port
4 medium tomatoes
Salt, pepper, chopped parsley

Place the ham in the blender, add the fromage frais and process until the mixture is smooth. Season with salt, pepper and chopped parsley. Beat the egg whites until they form stiff peaks and fold them gently into the mixture.

Soften the gelatine leaves in cold water and drain. Bring the port or madeira to the boil and dissolve the gelatine in it. Mix this liquid gently but thoroughly into the mixture and pour into a charlotte mould.

Leave to set in the refrigerator for 12 hours. Make a tomato coulis, using the recipe on page 77.

To serve, turn the mousse out of the mould and pour the coulis around it.

Asparagus bavarois
Bavarois d'asperges

Serves 4

Preparation: 15 minutes
Cooking time: 20 minutes
Refrigeration: 2 hours

Ingredients:

1 kg asparagus
300 ml semi-skimmed milk
3 leaves (1 sachet) gelatine
2 egg whites
1 tablespoon low-fat crème fraîche

Wash and peel the asparagus. Cut into small pieces, keeping a few of the tips to cook in salted water and use for decoration. Cook the rest of the asparagus in the milk for 20 minutes and then put both milk and cooked asparagus through a blender.

Soften the gelatine leaves in cold water and drain. Add it to the asparagus mixture. If using powdered gelatine, follow the instructions on the packet. Add the crème fraîche. Season with salt and pepper and leave to cool for a few minutes.

Beat the eggs until they form stiff peaks and then fold them gently into the mixture. Moisten the sides of four ramekins. Pour the mixture into them and place in the refrigerator to set for 2 hours.

To serve, turn out onto individual plates and garnish with the asparagus tips.

Suggestion:

Each bavarois can be served in the centre of the plate, decorated with a few asparagus tips and dressed with a teaspoonful of vinaigrette. The vinaigrette can be made with balsamic or sherry vinegar and olive oil.

Mushroom and garlic fromage frais mould
Flan d'ail au fromage blanc

Serves 4

Preparation: 10 minutes
Cooking time: 40 minutes

Ingredients:

200 g garlic
150 g fromage frais
100 g tinned button mushrooms
4 eggs
10 g butter
Salt, pepper

Peel the garlic cloves and remove the central shoot. Steam or cook in a very little water for 20 minutes. Purée the garlic and mushrooms together in a blender.

Add the fromage frais and season with salt and pepper. Mix thoroughly until the purée is smooth and creamy. Then add the beaten eggs and a dash of salt.

Place the mixture in buttered ramekins and cook in a bain-marie for 20 minutes at 180°C (350°F, gas mark 4). They are cooked when the tops feel firm to the touch.

Serve tepid, with a tomato and basil coulis (see page 77).

Bavarois of cucumber and fromage frais with a cucumber coulis
Bavarois de fromage blanc aux concombres et son coulis

Serves 6

Preparation: 30 minutes
Cooking time: 5 minutes
Refrigeration: 3 hours

Ingredients:

500 g fromage frais
200 ml milk
1 1/2 leaves (1/2 sachet) gelatine
400 g cucumber, plus
cucumber for the coulis
200 g tomatoes
10 fresh mint leaves
Salt, pepper

Wash the tomatoes, plunge into boiling water for 30 seconds, skin and remove the seeds. Peel the cucumbers, putting half a cucumber aside for the coulis. Cover the tomatoes and cucumbers with rough salt and leave for 1 hour to draw out the liquid. Chop half the fresh mint and mix with the fromage frais, with salt and pepper to season.

Soften the gelatine leaves in cold water and drain. Heat the milk and dissolve the gelatine in it. Combine the milk gently with the fromage frais.

Rinse and drain the cucumber and tomatoes. Chop these into small pieces and add to the fromage frais mixture. Place in a loaf tin and allow to set in a refrigerator for 3 hours.

Make a coulis by blending the reserved half-cucumber and the remaining mint leaves. Season with salt and pepper.

Turn out the bavarois immediately before serving and pour the coulis over it.

Suggestion:

The mint can be replaced with basil and the cucumber coulis by one made from tomatoes and basil.

71

Crab, fish and avocado loaf
Pain de surimi

Serves 6

Preparation: 30 minutes
Cooking time: 3 minutes
Refrigeration: 12 hours

Ingredients:

400 g frozen fish sticks
("crab sticks", "ocean sticks")
2 avocados
4 hard-boiled eggs
4 tablespoons thick low-fat
crème fraîche
4 tablespoons chopped chervil
1 tin crab pieces
2 leaves (or 2 teaspoons powdered)
gelatine
Juice of 1 lemon
1 teaspoon olive oil
Salt, pepper

Thaw the fish sticks in the refrigerator. Peel the avocados and remove the stones. Blend the flesh of the avocados with 2 tablespoons of the crème fraîche. Season with the lemon juice, salt, pepper and chervil.

Oil a loaf tin and line the bottom and sides with fish sticks. Reserve some to place on the top of the loaf. Chop the remainder of the fish sticks and the hard-boiled eggs.

Soften the gelatine leaves in cold water and drain. Heat the rest of the crème fraîche and dissolve the gelatine in it.

Mix the chopped fish sticks and chopped egg together and combine with half the warm crème fraîche. Leave to cool until lukewarm.

Drain the crab and add it to the remainder of the warm crème fraîche. Stir and leave to cool until lukewarm. Into the loaf tin pour a layer of the fish sticks mixture, followed by a layer of avocado mixture, a layer of crab mixture, a second layer of avocado mixture and, finally, a second layer of fish sticks mixture.

Place the remaining fish sticks on top and refrigerate for 12 hours.

Poultry terrine
Terrine de volaille

Serves 8

Preparation: 20 minutes
Cooking time: 2 hours

Ingredients:

500 g chicken breasts (turkey or rabbit can be used)
200 g pork
100 g mild cooked ham
2 eggs
1 onion
5 shallots
120 ml cognac
Thyme, parsley
Salt, pepper

Steam the chicken and pork. Blend with the ham, onion and shallots to form a mixture the consistency of stuffing.

Season with thyme and parsley. Add the glass of cognac and the eggs, lightly beaten. Mix well and season with salt and pepper.

Place the mixture in a terrine. Cook in a bain-marie in an oven set to 200°C (400°F, gas mark 6) for 2 hours.

Allow to cool before turning out.

Terrine of poultry liver
Terrine de foies de volailles

Serves 8

Preparation: 20 minutes
Cooking time: 2 hours

Ingredients:

750 g poultry livers
500 g sausage meat
4 shallots
2 cloves garlic
Small bunch chervil
A few leaves tarragon
3 eggs
1 liqueur glass armagnac
A few rashers of bacon
Salt, pepper

Chop the livers and mix with the sausage meat. Peel the garlic and shallots and chop finely, together with the bunch of chervil and the tarragon leaves.

Combine with the livers and sausage meat and season with salt and pepper. Add the eggs, lightly beaten, and the armagnac and mix thoroughly until smooth.

Line the bottom and sides of a terrine with rashers of bacon. Transfer the mixture to the dish, pressing it down well. Decorate the top with pieces of bacon and further tarragon leaves.

Cover and cook in a hot oven (220° C, 425°F, gas mark 7) for two hours.

Allow to cool completely before serving.

Mousse of Parma ham and leeks
Mousse de Parme aux poireaux

Serves 6

Preparation: 20 minutes
Cooking time: 40 minutes

Ingredients:

2 kg leeks (white part only)
200 g very thinly sliced
Parma ham
1 bunch chives
30 g butter
2 eggs
100 g grated cheese
Salt, pepper
100 ml low-fat crème fraîche

Wash the leeks, blanch for 10 minutes in boiling salted water and drain.

Blend the Parma ham and add the eggs, lightly beaten, the cream and the grated cheese. Season with the salt, pepper and chopped chives.

Pour a layer of the mixture into a loaf tin and follow this with a layer of leeks. Continue in this way until the tin is filled.

Place in the oven at 220°C (425°F, gas mark 7) for 30 minutes. Serve in slices, hot or cold.

Suggestion:

The discarded green parts of the leeks can be used in a vegetable soup.

Salmon and spinach terrine
Terrine d'épinards au saumon

Serves 4

Preparation: 30 minutes
Cooking time: 10 minutes
Refrigeration: 2 to 3 hours

Ingredients:

200 g spinach
200 g fresh salmon fillet
(with skin removed)
200 g single cream
2 tablespoons olive oil
1 1/2 leaves (or 1/2 sachet) gelatine
200 ml low-fat crème fraîche for
the dressing
2 limes
Salt, pepper

Wash the spinach, remove the stalks and chop the leaves finely. Cook in the olive oil over a low heat. Blend the raw salmon with the cooked spinach until very smooth.

Soften the gelatine in cold water and drain. Whip the cream until quite stiff (the consistency of Chantilly). Take 2 table-spoons of the whipped cream and heat gently in a saucepan. Dissolve the gelatine in the cream.

Add this mixture to the spinach and salmon purée. Fold in the rest of the whipped cream and season.

Line a fairly shallow dish with aluminium foil. Pour the mixture in and cover tightly with a further sheet of foil. Leave in a refrigerator for 2 to 3 hours to set.

Serve the terrine in slices, accompanied by low-fat crème fraîche and garnished with slices of lime.

Cucumber sorbet served with a tomato coulis
Concombre en sorbet et coulis de tomates

Serves 4

Preparation: 10 minutes
Refrigeration: 3 1/2 hours

Ingredients:

1 cucumber
2 full cream yogurts
8 fresh mint leaves
2 firm tomatoes
Juice of 1 lemon
Salt

Peel the cucumber, slice it in half lengthways, cover with rough salt and set aside to draw out the liquid. Drain, remove the seeds and blend the cucumber flesh with the mint leaves, yogurt and salt.

Pour the mixture into ice-cube trays and leave in the freezer for 3 hours.

Plunge the tomatoes into very hot water for 30 seconds, skin and remove the seeds. Allow to drain, then blend with the lemon juice to make the tomato coulis. Season with salt.

Crush the frozen cubes into fine flakes in a blender. Pack into a mould and return to the freezer for a further half-hour.

Serve the sorbet, using an ice-cream scoop, with the tomato coulis.

Cucumber with fennel, mint and yogurt dressing
Concombre au yaourt et menthe

Serves 6

Preparation: 30 minutes

Ingredients:

3 cucumbers
3 natural yogurts
1 teaspoon chopped fresh fennel
3 tablespoons olive oil
1 teaspoon chopped fresh mint
1 teaspoon salt
2 tablespoons wine vinegar
2 cloves garlic

Peel the cucumbers, slice them in two, remove the pips and seeds and chop into small pieces. Cover with rough salt to draw out the liquid and leave for 15 minutes.

Crush the garlic and place in a bowl with the vinegar. Leave to marinate for 10 minutes. Then, in another bowl, mix the yogurt, olive oil and fennel.

Pour the vinegar through a fine sieve and add to the yogurt mixture. Drain the cucumber thoroughly, rinse and dry.

Serve the cucumber with the yogurt dressing, sprinkled with chopped mint.

Artichokes bottoms with fromage frais and Roquefort
Artichauts au fromage blanc

Serves 6

Preparation: 40 minutes
Cooking time: 20-25 minutes

Ingredients:

6 artichokes (or ready-to-use artichoke bottoms)
125 g Roquefort
5 tablespoons fromage frais
1 lemon
2-3 tablespoons low-fat crème fraîche
Salt, pepper, nutmeg

Trim the artichokes and retain only the bases. (At this stage, however, you can leave the hairy choke, which is more easily removed after cooking.)

Dip the artichoke bottoms in lemon juice to prevent discoloration. Then cook in boiling salted water, with the lemon juice added.

Keep an eye on the cooking time; the artichokes should remain firm and are cooked when they can be pierced with a pointed knife. Drain and allow to cool, removing the choke.

Crumble the Roquefort and mix with the fromage frais and the crème fraîche. Whip the mixture to thicken it and season with pepper, nutmeg and a dash of salt.

Pile the mixture onto the individual artichoke bottoms and serve.

Tomatoes stuffed with tuna
Tomates au thon

Serves 6

Preparation: 30 minutes

Ingredients:

6 medium tomatoes
200 gm tuna in brine
500 g fresh peas
200 ml sunflower oil
1 tablespoon olive oil
1 teaspoon Dijon mustard
2 garlic cloves
1 egg yolk
1 tablespoon chopped parsley
Salt, pepper

Slice off the round end of the tomatoes, scoop out the inside with a small spoon (keep the flesh), and turn them upside down to drain.

Shell the peas and cook in boiling salted water for 2 minutes. Drain and allow to cool.

Make a mayonnaise, as follows:

Crush 3 cloves of garlic and combine with the egg yolk and mustard. Whisk in, a very little at a time, the 20cl sunflower oil, and then the tablespoonful of olive oil. Season with salt and pepper.

Drain and flake the tuna. Combine with the mayonnaise, peas and drained tomato flesh. Fill the tomatoes with the mixture, sprinkle with chopped parsley and replace the lids. Serve chilled.

Aubergine caviar
Caviar d'aubergines

Serves 6

Preparation: 25 minutes
Cooking time: 1 hour

Ingredients:

4 aubergines
2 tomatoes
4 tablespoons olive oil
1 bouquet garni (parsley, thyme, bay)
1 clove garlic
2 shallots
Salt, pepper

Wash and dry the aubergines, slice them in two and make light cuts in the flesh inside.

Place in an ovenproof dish, season with salt and pepper and drizzle a little olive oil over them. Bake in a hot oven (200°C, 400°F, gas mark 6) for 30 minutes. Remove from the oven when cooked and scrape out the insides to recover the "caviar" (the flesh and seeds).

Plunge the tomatoes into boiling water for 30 seconds, skin and remove the seeds.

Fry the garlic and chopped shallots gently in a tablespoon of olive oil. Then add the tomatoes, chopped, and the bouquet garni and simmer for 10 minutes. Remove the bouquet garni.

Season with salt and pepper. Add the aubergine "caviar" and cook very gently for a further half-hour.

Blend the mixture, so as to obtain a purée, and allow to cool. Serve well chilled.

Salad of mixed summer vegetables
Salade du jardinier

Serves 6

Preparation: 1 hour
Cooking time: 25 minutes
Refrigeration: 20-30 minutes

Ingredients:

1 kg short asparagus (white or green type)
250 g French beans
Half a raw cauliflower
1 cucumber
1 bunch radishes
1 lettuce
1 medium onion
1 bunch chervil
2 sprigs tarragon
1 bunch watercress

For the vinaigrette:

4 tablespoons olive oil
1 tablespoon vinegar
Salt, pepper

Cook the beans for about 12 minutes, so they are still firm, and cut them into pieces a few centimetres long. Do the same with the asparagus, first peeling the stalks as necessary.

Wash the cucumber but do not peel. Slice thinly. Break the cauliflower into florets and blanch for 2 minutes in boiling water.

Make a vinaigrette and add the chopped chervil, tarragon, watercress leaves and onion.

Wash the lettuce and shred the heart. Slice half the radishes. Mix all the ingredients together in the vinaigrette and leave in the refrigerator for 20 to 30 minutes for the flavours to mingle.

Garnish with the rest of the radishes and serve.

Green salad with bacon and saucisson
Salade au saucisson

Serves 6

Preparation: 20 minutes
Cooking time: 25 minutes

Ingredients:

1 good-sized head of curly endive
300 g streaky bacon
(in a piece, not rashers)
1 saucisson de Lyon (200 g)
or other large cooking sausage
Olive oil
Wine vinegar
Salt, pepper

Cook the saucisson de Lyon gently in salted water for 20 minutes. (Or cook according to the type of sausage you are using.) Wash and spin the curly endive.

Blanch the bacon in boiling water for 5 minutes, drain it on absorbent kitchen paper and dice it. Fry gently in a pan.

Make a vinaigrette and toss the salad in it. Place slices of sausage and the diced bacon on top.

Serve right away.

Egg, tuna and prawn salad with paprika dressing
Salade paprika

Serves 6

Preparation: 20 minutes
Cooking time: 3 minutes

Ingredients:

1 good-sized lettuce
6 tomatoes
3 hard-boiled eggs
200 g tinned tuna in brine
200 g frozen peeled prawns
400 g fresh button mushrooms
Juice of 1 lemon

For the vinaigrette:

3-4 tablespoons olive oil
1-2 tablespoons wine vinegar
1 tablespoon paprika
Mustard, salt, pepper

Trim the mushrooms as necessary, wash thoroughly under cold water and drain. Slice thinly into a dish and sprinkle with lemon juice.

If the frozen prawns are uncooked, plunge them into well salted boiling water for 3 minutes and then rinse in cold water.

Use scissors to shred the lettuce. Slice the tomatoes and cut the eggs into quarters. Drain and flake the tuna. Put all the ingredients into a salad-bowl.

Make a vinaigrette of olive oil, vinegar, mustard, salt and pepper and stir the paprika into it.

Serve the vinaigrette separately.

White cabbage salad with bacon
Salade de chou blanc aux lardons

Serves 8

Preparation: 30 minutes
Cooking time: 5 minutes

Ingredients:

1 large hard white cabbage
400 g smoked streaky bacon
(in a piece not rashers)
5 hard-boiled eggs
Chopped parsley

For the vinaigrette:

Olive oil
Vinegar
Mustard, salt, pepper

Remove the outside leaves and wash the cabbage under running water. Dry with a cloth or absorbent kitchen paper.

Halve or quarter the cabbage and shred finely, using a sharp knife.

Cut the hard-boiled eggs in half and remove the yolks. Make the yolks into a "mimosa", using a "moulinette" if you have one. Cut the whites into little cubes or thin strips.

Dice the bacon, discarding the ends if they are very fat. Fry very gently in a non-stick pan, greased with a little olive oil.

Make a classic vinaigrette from olive oil, mustard, vinegar, salt and pepper.

Transfer the cabbage first to the serving dish or individual plates. Scatter the egg whites over it and then sprinkle with the "mimosa" of egg yolks and the chopped parsley. Season with the vinaigrette.

Add the hot diced bacon at the last minute.

Oriental salad
Salade orientale

Serves 4

Preparation: 20 minutes

Ingredients:

150 g beansprouts
1/2 cucumber
100 g white cabbage
100 g red cabbage

For the vinaigrette:

2 tablespoons wine vinegar
1 tablespoon olive oil
1 tablespoon bottled soy sauce
Salt, pepper

Wash and drain the vegetables. Shred the cabbage finely with a very sharp knife. Peel the cucumber and dice it.

Make a vinaigrette from the oil, vinegar, soy sauce, salt and pepper.

Mingle the vegetables together in the vinaigrette and serve chilled.

Salad of beansprouts and scampi
Salade de soja aux langoustines

Serves 6 to 8

Preparation: 45 minutes
Cooking time: 20 minutes

Ingredients:

500 g beansprouts
300 g fresh button mushrooms
250 g frozen peas
6 small tomatoes
1 bunch radishes
Juice of 2 lemons
16-20 (1 kg) scampi (Dublin
Bay prawns, langoustines)
100 g black olives

For the vinaigrette:

Olive oil
Wine vinegar
1 onion
1 clove garlic
Salt, pepper

Wash the beansprouts and blanch for 3 minutes in boiling salted water. Rinse in cold water and drain.

Cook the scampi for 5 minutes in boiling salted water. Rinse immediately in cold water and shell. Keep a few for decoration and break the others into pieces.

Trim the mushrooms as necessary, rinse in water containing lemon juice and slice thinly.

Cook the peas in boiling salted water. Then make a vinaigrette with 5 tablespoons of olive oil, 1 tablespoon of vinegar, the (finely chopped) onion, the (crushed) garlic, salt and pepper. Toss all the vegetables and the other ingredients in the vinaigrette and leave for 20 to 30 minutes for the flavours to mingle.

Before serving, garnish with the reserved scampi, the washed and trimmed radishes, the tomatoes cut in quarters and the black olives.

Greek salad
Salade grecque

Serves 4

Preparation: 15 minutes

Ingredients:

1 cucumber
4 tomatoes
1 fresh white onion
or 1 red onion
2 small green peppers
150 g feta
24 black olives
1 tablespoon chopped parsley
or a few leaves basil

For the vinaigrette:

2 tablespoons olive oil
1 tablespoon wine vinegar
Salt, pepper

Wash and quarter the tomatoes. Peel the cucumber and cut into medium thick slices. Do the same with the onion.

Remove the stalk ends from the peppers, pare thinly with a potato peeler, remove the seeds and cut into pieces.

Make a vinaigrette from the olive oil, wine vinegar, salt and pepper. Toss the salad ingredients in the vinaigrette and transfer to individual plates.

Serve with slices of feta and black olives, and garnished with chopped parsley.

Seafood salad
Salade marine

Serves 6

Preparation: 30 minutes
Cooking time: 30 minutes

Ingredients:

500 g squid
1/2 litre mussels
1/2 litre cockles
120 ml dry white wine
1 head escarole, frisée or cos
3 tomatoes
Juice of 1 lemon
Olive oil
Chopped fines herbes
Salt, pepper

Use ready-prepared squid. Clean it and cut into strips. Cook for 15 to 20 minutes in boiling water. Drain and dry.

Wash the cockles. Heat the white wine and plunge the cockles into it, on a high heat, so that they open up. Remove from their shells and drain. (Keep the liquid.)

Again over a high heat, open the mussels and remove from their shells. Make a sauce consisting of two thirds liquid reserved from the cockles to one third olive oil, adding the lemon juice, chopped fines herbes, salt and pepper. Pour this over the seafood and leave for 20 to 30 minutes.

Shred the lettuce and transfer to the salad-bowl. Just before serving, pour the shellfish on top and garnish with tomato quarters.

Sliced duck breast with leek and raspberries
Salade au magret de canard

Serves 2

Preparation: 25 minutes
Cooking time: 30 minutes

Ingredients:

1 leek (white part)
2 tablespoons sunflower oil
1 magret de canard
1 tablespoon raspberry vinegar
120 ml red wine
2 tablespoons raspberries
Nutmeg
Salt, pepper

Wash the leek and cut into thin slices. Fry until golden in sunflower oil on a high heat and season with salt, pepper and grated nutmeg.

Cook the magret de canard (duck breast) in a frying pan, on a high heat, fat side first, until it is really crispy. Remove from pan and set aside.

Remove the excess fat from the pan and then add the vinegar. Allow to simmer for a few minutes. Then add the red wine and allow to reduce further.

Arrange the leek in a circle on the plates. Slice the magret thinly and arrange on top.

Immediately before serving, pour the sauce over it and decorate with fresh raspberries.

Eggs in aspic
Aspic d'œufs

Serves 6

Preparation: 30 minutes
Cooking time: 3 to 4 minutes
Refrigeration: 3 to 4 hours

Ingredients:

12 eggs
1/4 litre aspic (made from aspic jelly powder)
2 thin slices cooked ham
White vinegar
Chives

Pour 1 cm of jelly into each of six ramekins and set in refrigerator.

Chop the chives roughly and cut the ham into diamond shapes. Soft boil the eggs (5 minutes) in water with a little vinegar added and allow to cool.

Place the eggs in the ramekins with a little chive and cover with a slice of ham. Pour the rest of the jelly over and leave in the refrigerator to set for 3 to 4 hours.

To serve, turn out onto a dish garnished with lettuce.

Eggs stuffed with tuna, anchovies or tapenade
Œufs farcis mimosa

Serves 6

Preparation: 30 minutes
Cooking time: 10 minutes

Ingredients:

12 eggs
150 g black olives
1 small tin anchovy fillets in oil
1 small tin tuna in oil
2 tablespoons tapenade
1 tablespoon chopped fines herbes
Olive oil
Salt, pepper

Boil the eggs for 10 minutes. Cut in half lengthways and remove the yolks. Put the yolks through a "moulinette" or crumble with a fork. Reserve two tablespoons of the crumbled yolk for decoration.

Divide the rest of the yolk into three:

Break up the tuna and combine with the first portion of egg yolk, adding a pinch of fines herbes and a few drop of oil from the tin of tuna.

Process the anchovy fillets, combine with the second portion of egg yolk and season with fines herbes and a few drops of oil from the tin.

Combine the tapenade with the third portion of egg yolk.

Divide the egg white halves into three groups, filling a third with the tuna mixture, a third with the anchovy mixture and a third with the tapenade mixture.

Sprinkle with the reserved crumbled egg yolk and garnish with black olives.

Note:

Tapenade is a Provençal paste made from olives, anchovies and capers. It is available ready-made at many British delicatessens.

A ring of baked eggs served with a mixed salad
Œufs en couronne

Serves 6

Preparation: 10 minutes
Cooking time: 10 minutes

Ingredients:

12 eggs
10 g butter for the mould

300 g mixed salad ingredients:

Parma ham, gruyère, celeriac or French beans, frozen squid, peppers, shallots, tomatoes and vinaigrette.

Take a 20-22 cm savarin mould and butter it. Make a bain-marie and place the mould in it (the water should reach to half-way up the mould).

Break the eggs one at a time into the mould and season with salt and pepper. Place in the oven at 200°C (400°F, gas mark 6) for 10 minutes. (The yolks should remain soft.)

Allow to cool, use the blade of a knife to help release from the sides of the mould and turn out onto a serving dish. Make up a mixed salad, as follows:

Cut the ham and peppers into strips, the gruyère into cubes, the celeriac or French beans into thin sticks and the tomatoes into quarters.

Cut the squid into strips and sweat with the shallots in olive oil for 2 to 3 minutes. Add to the other salad ingredients.

To serve, season the salad and arrange it in the centre of the egg ring.

White fish soufflé served with watercress sauce
Soufflé de poisson cressonnière

Serves 6

Preparation: 20 minutes
Cooking time: 25 minutes

Ingredients:

200 g white fish fillets
4 eggs
6 tablespoons crème fraîche
25 g butter
2 teaspoons lemon juice
2 tablespoons chopped fresh parsley

For the sauce:

1 bunch watercress
6 tablespoons white wine
2 tablespoons whipped cream
Salt, pepper
2 shallots

Clean the fish fillets, washing in cold water and patting dry with absorbent kitchen paper. Process, adding the egg yolks and crème fraîche. Season with the lemon juice, salt and pepper.

Beat the egg whites until they form stiff peaks and fold them very gently into the mixture so that they do not collapse.

Butter straight-sided individual moulds and fill with the mixture. Cook in an oven set at 180°C (350°F, gas mark 4) for 20 minutes. Turn the oven up to 200°C (400°F, gas mark 6) and cook for a further 5 minutes.

Meanwhile, prepare the sauce, as follows:

Reduce the watercress and shallots in the white wine for a few minutes on a high heat. Put the mixture through a blender and return to the pan to thicken over a low heat.

Put the mixture through a fine sieve to obtain a smooth sauce. Stir in the whipped cream and season with salt and pepper.

Serve the soufflés on individual plates accompanied by the sauce.

Tuna and olive spread
Purée de thon aux olives

Serves 4

Preparation: 10 minutes

Ingredients:

200 g tuna in brine
100 g black olives, pitted
50 g capers
1 tablespoon low-fat crème fraîche
2 egg yolks
1 clove garlic
Olive oil
Salt, pepper, Cayenne pepper

Drain the tuna. Peel the garlic. Put the tuna, stoned olives, capers, egg yolks, garlic and crème fraîche through the blender.

Add olive oil gradually until a smooth paste is obtained. Taste, add salt if necessary, and season with pepper and Cayenne.

Refrigerate.

Suggestions:

The spread can be used to fill celery or chicory leaves for a party buffet, or to garnish small raw tomatoes, hard-boiled egg whites, cooked artichoke bases or mushrooms.

Tuna in aspic with mushrooms and fromage frais dressing
Thon en gelée

Serves 6

Preparation: 15 minutes
Refrigeration: 6 hours

Ingredients:

600 g tinned tuna in brine
1 sachet aspic jelly powder
6-8 bay leaves
1 bunch parsley
1 bunch chives
200 g small button mushrooms, fresh
250 g fromage frais
Juice of 1 lemon
1 sprig fresh fennel
Olive oil
Salt, pepper

Make the aspic according to the instructions on the packet and pour a little into a savarin mould. Lay the bay leaves on the aspic and place in the refrigerator to set.

Drain and flake the tuna. Place it in the mould, on top of the bay leaves. Add the parsley and chives, chopped, and the rest of the aspic. Leave in the refrigerator to set for 6 hours.

Trim the mushrooms as necessary. Wash and season with olive oil, lemon juice, salt and pepper.

Make a dressing to accompany the dish, by mixing the fromage frais with lemon juice, chopped fennel, salt and pepper.

Turn out the tuna in aspic onto a serving dish, place the mushrooms in the centre and serve with the sauce.

Salmon fillets in white fish mousse with mayonnaise
Mousse de saumon

Serves 8-10

Preparation: 30 minutes
Cooking time: 1 1/2 hours

Ingredients:

1 kg fresh salmon fillets
1 kg coley (or cod) fillets
4 egg whites
100 g low-fat crème fraîche
200 g mayonnaise
1 handful sorrel
Salt, pepper

For the mayonnaise:

1 egg yolk
1 teaspoon mustard
200 ml oil
A little vinegar
Salt, pepper

Clean the coley (or cod) fillets, put them through the blender and season with salt and pepper. Then add the crème fraîche.

Beat the egg whites until they form stiff peaks and fold them gently into the mixture.

Line a loaf tin with aluminium foil. Place a layer of the coley (or cod) mixture in the bottom. On top place some of the salmon fillets, cut as necessary, and repeat the operation until the mould has been filled. Cook in bain-marie in a gentle oven (150° C, 300°F, gas mark 2) for 1 hour.

Make a classic mayonnaise with sunflower oil, adding a tablespoon of olive oil.

Turn out the mousse and serve cold with the mayonnaise.

Individual salmon and mint moulds
Pâtés de saumon à la menthe

Serves 4

Preparation: 1 hour
Cooking time: 20 minutes
Refrigeration: 12 hours

Ingredients:

1 slice smoked salmon
500 g fresh salmon fillet
2-3 tablespoons fresh mint
1 leaf (or 1 teaspoon powdered) gelatine
1 tablespoon low-fat crème fraîche
1 large courgette
Olive oil
Salt, pepper

Cook the fresh salmon fillet, wrapped in paper or foil parcels, in the oven for 30 minutes or wrap in foil and steam. Allow to cool.

Wash and chop the fresh mint. Wash the courgette and slice thinly lengthwise, leaving the skin on.

Fry the courgette slices in olive oil until golden (30 seconds on each side, on a high heat). Leave to cool on kitchen paper. Flake the cooked salmon roughly and chop the smoked salmon.

Soften the gelatine leaves in cold water and drain. Heat the olive oil gently and add the gelatine leaves. Combine this liquid with the salmon and add the crème fraîche and mint. Mix well together and season with salt and pepper.

Line 4 ramekins with slices of courgette and pour the mixture in. Leave for 12 hours in the refrigerator. Remove thirty minutes before serving and turn out at the last minute.

Terrine of salmon trout with a fennel coulis
Terrine de truite au fenouil

Serves 4

Preparation: 1 hour
Cooking time: 20 minutes
Refrigeration: 12 hours

Ingredients:

1 small salmon trout (about 1 kg)
200 ml low-fat crème fraîche
1/4 litre aspic (made from aspic jelly powder)
2 sprigs thyme
3 bay leaves
1 large onion spiked with 3 cloves
1 clove garlic
600 g fennel
1 lime
2 tablespoons olive oil
1 bunch dill
Salt, peppercorns

Cook the trout in a court-bouillon, by using the salt, peppercorns, the onion spiked with cloves, bay, thyme and the clove of garlic in the cooking water.

From the moment the water boils, allow 10 minutes over a low heat. Remove from the heat and allow trout to cool in the court-bouillon.

Clean the fennel, removing any stalks which are too tough. Cut each stalk in two and cook in the pressure cooker for 10 minutes. Pour the cooking liquid through a sieve and use it to make the aspic, following the instructions on the packet.

Skin and bone the fish and break up the flesh with a fork. Allow the aspic to cool slightly before adding half of it to the fish and putting the mixture through the blender. Then add the remainder of the aspic, the cream and salt and pepper to season.

Moisten a loaf tin, transfer the mixture to it and leave in the refrigerator to set for 12 hours.

Crush the fennel in the food processor, adding the lemon juice. Strain the purée through a sieve to make a coulis and season with salt, pepper and finely chopped dill. Chill.

Remove the mousse from the refrigerator 15 minutes before serving, turn out at the last minute and serve in thick slices with the fennel coulis.

Fish loaf
Pain de poisson

Serves 6

Preparation: 15 minutes
Cooking time: 40 minutes

Ingredients:

600 g hake fillets
2 or 3 ripe tomatoes
6 eggs
4 cloves garlic
1 bunch basil
4 tablespoons olive oil
Salt, pepper

Plunge the tomatoes into boiling water for 30 seconds, skin and remove the seeds. Fry gently with the crushed garlic in the olive oil until all the liquid disappears.

Blend the raw hake fillets and add the tomato purée, the eggs (lightly beaten), the basil leaves (chopped), salt and pepper.

Oil a loaf tin, pour the mixture in and cook in a bain-marie in a moderate oven (180°C, 35°F, gas mark 4) for 40 minutes.

Turn out and serve tepid or cold, with an olive oil mayonnaise or a tomato coulis.

Pike and vegetable mould
Flan de sandre aux légumes

Serves 6

Preparation: 25 minutes
Cooking time: 40 minutes

Ingredients:

600 g fresh perch or pike
50 g fresh French beans
50 g peas
2 eggs, plus 2 egg whites
200 g fromage frais
3 tablespoons low-fat crème fraîche
Salt, pepper

Put the pike fillets through the blender. Add the eggs one at a time, followed by the egg whites, beating continuously. Then add the fromage frais and the crème fraîche. Season with salt and pepper.

Boil the French beans for 5 minutes and cut them into pieces. Add them to the mixture, together with the peas.

Butter a loaf tin and pour the mixture in. Cook in a bain-marie in a hot oven (210°C, 420°F, gas mark 6-7) for 40 minutes. Serve hot or cold.

Note:

The original French version of the recipe uses zander, a river fish rarely found in Britain. It will work very well using perch (if available) or pike instead.

Salad of spinach and cockles
Salade d'épinards aux coques

Serves 6

Preparation: 30 minutes
Cooking time: 10 minutes

Ingredients:

1.4 kg cockles
800 g spinach
200 ml white wine
200 g whipping cream
3 tomatoes
1 shallot
Nutmeg
Sherry vinegar
Chives
Paprika

Rinse the cockles several times and dry them. Heat the white wine with the shallot and add the cockles, on a high heat, so that they open up. Remove from their shells.

Trim and wash the spinach. Cook half of it in boiling salted water for 5 minutes. Drain and put through the blender, with the salt, pepper, nutmeg and sherry vinegar.

Whip the cream until stiff (like Chantilly), then fold it into the spinach mixture. Chop the remainder of the raw spinach finely.

Place the spinach mixture in the centre of the plate, add the cockles and surround with the raw spinach.

Garnish with tomato quarters and sprinkle with chives and paprika. Serve immediately.

Skate served on a bed of salad
Raie en salade

Serves 6

Preparation: 15 minutes
Cooking time: 10 minutes

Ingredients:

1.2 kg skate wings
120 ml capers
1 tin red peppers
1 head curly endive
1 cos lettuce
A few sprigs thyme
1 bay leaf
2 lemons

For the vinaigrette:

2 tablespoons sherry vinegar
1 tablespoon hazelnut oil
5 tablespoons olive oil
Salt, pepper

Remove the grey skin from the skate wings and cook the fish in water to which the juice of 2 lemons, the thyme, bay leaf and salt have been added.

Allow five minutes from the time the water boils; then remove from the heat and allow fish to cool in the cooking liquid. Remove the remaining white skin.

Wash and spin the salad and shred it. Take the skate wings and detach the flesh from the cartilage. Place the green salad on a serving dish and arrange the fish on top. Add the capers and the peppers (diced).

Make a vinaigrette with 1 tablespoon of hazelnut oil, 5 tablespoons of olive oil, 2 tablespoons of sherry vinegar, salt and pepper.

Serve the dish dressed with the vinaigrette.

Sardines served with celery and cucumber salad
Sardines en salade

Serves 6

Preparation: 30 minutes
Cooking time: 10 minutes

Ingredients:

12 good-sized fresh sardines
2 red peppers
100 ml olive oil
1 cucumber
1 head celery
24 black olives
3 sprigs thyme
2 bay leaves
2 lemons
Salt, pepper

Gut the sardines, wash and dry. Slit them along the back to remove the backbone.

Bake the peppers in the oven, peel them and cut each into 12 strips. Place a strip inside each sardine and transfer to an ovenproof dish.

Chop the bay leaf and thyme finely and mix with the olive oil and lemon juice. Pour this mixture over the sardines and place in a very hot oven (use 300ºC, 475ºF, gas mark 9, or the hottest setting available on your oven) for 10 minutes.

Peel and finely dice the cucumber. Wash and chop the celery heart.

Serve the sardines warm, garnished with black olives and slices of lemon and accompanied by the cucumber and celery.

Celeriac and mussels in a rémoulade sauce
Céleri aux moules

Serves 4

Preparation: 20 minutes
Cooking time: 10 minutes
Refrigeration: 12 hours

Ingredients:

1 small root celeriac
1 litre mussels
1 tablespoon strong mustard
1 shallot
1 egg yolk
1 spoonful olive oil
200 ml sunflower oil
1 tablespoon chopped parsley
120 ml dry white wine
Salt, pepper

Clean the mussels. Heat the white wine and, on a high heat, stir the mussels in it for 3 minutes so that they open up. Remove the shells and reserve the liquid. Peel the celeriac and dice it.

Cook the celeriac in the pressure-cooker, using the liquid from the mussels. Allow three minutes from the time the cooker reaches full pressure.

Make a rémoulade sauce, as follows:

Mix together the mustard, salt and pepper and gradually add 200 ml of sunflower oil and one tablespoon of olive oil to make a mayonnaise.

Chop the shallot finely and stir into the mayonnaise. Then stir the celeriac and mussels into the sauce and leave in the refrigerator for 12 hours for the flavours to develop.

To serve, sprinkle with chopped parsley.

Mussels served on a bed of green salad
Salade de moules

Serves 6

Preparation: 30 minutes
Cooking time: 10 minutes
Refrigeration: 30 minutes

Ingredients:

1.5 litres mussels
1 medium onion, finely chopped
1 head curly endive
1 tablespoon olive oil
1/2 teaspoon thyme leaves

For the dressing:

2 cloves garlic
15-20 leaves basil
6 tablespoons olive oil
1 tablespoon wine vinegar
Salt, pepper

Place the olive oil over a high heat and in it fry the onion until golden, along with the thyme. Add the mussels so that they open up and remove from their shells.

Next, prepare the dressing. Crush the garlic and add the oil at a trickle, stirring continuously to obtain a smooth mixture. Then add the vinegar, salt and pepper.

Stir the mussels into the dressing and leave to marinate for 30 minutes in the refrigerator. Serve on a bed of curly endive.

Salad of avocados
and artichoke bottoms with crab
Salade au crabe

Serves 6 to 8

Preparation: 15 minutes
Cooking time: 5 minutes

Ingredients:

1 large (300 g) tin of crab
2 avocados
4 artichokes
2 sticks celery
1 lettuce
2 lemons

For the dressing:

1 egg yolk
Sunflower oil
1/2 tablespoon mustard
4 tablespoons low-fat crème fraîche
2 teaspoons chopped parsley
Salt, pepper

Wash and drain the lettuce. Trim the artichoke bottoms, remove the hairy choke and dip in lemon juice to prevent discoloration. Cut into strips and cook in boiling salted water for 5 minutes. Once cooked, place under cold running water and drain.

Remove the stones from the avocados and shape the flesh into little balls, using a melon-baller. Pour lemon juice over them to prevent discoloration.

Cut the celery sticks into small pieces and mingle all the salad ingredients with the crab.

Make a mayonnaise, using sunflower oil, and add the crème fraîche and the chopped parsley. Season with salt and pepper.

Serve the crab salad dressed with the mayonnaise.

Baked spinach and clams with a cheese topping
Palourdes gratinées aux épinards

Serves 6

Preparation: 20 minutes
Cooking time: 25 minutes

Ingredients:

2 kg clams
2 finely sliced shallots
500 g spinach
3 tablespoons olive oil
200 g crème fraîche
with 40% fat content
50 g grated Emmenthal cheese
Salt, pepper

Rinse the clams under running water. Place over a high heat, together with the shallots, for 5 minutes so that they open up. Remove from their shells.

Remove the spinach stalks and blanch for 5 minutes in boiling salted water.

Drain very thoroughly, chop roughly and fry in the olive oil, on a high heat, for 5 minutes.

Mix together the spinach, the clams and the crème fraîche. Pour this mixture into a gratin dish, sprinkle with grated Emmenthal and place in a hot oven (220°C, 425°F, gas mark 7) for 10 minutes.

Serve hot.

MAIN COURSE DISHES

Kidney omelette
Omelette aux rognons

Serves 6

Preparation: 30 minutes
Cooking time: 25 minutes

Ingredients:

12 eggs
1 veal or ox kidney (200-300 g)
3 tablespoons sunflower oil
100 g low-fat crème fraîche
1 teaspoon mustard
2 shallots
Salt, pepper

Clean and trim the kidney of its core and cut into large pieces. Fry over a high heat in a tablespoon of sunflower oil, until sealed but pink inside.

Remove from the heat, season with salt and pepper and set aside where it will keep warm without cooking further.

Slice the shallots finely and fry them in the same pan. Add a teaspoon of mustard and the crème fraîche. Cook on a medium heat until the sauce thickens.

Return the kidney pieces to the pan and stir into the sauce.

In another pan, make the omelette, using the rest of the sunflower oil. When it is cooked, place the kidneys in their sauce in the centre and fold the omelette over.

Serve at once.

Tuna omelette
Omelette au thon

Serves 4

Preparation: 10 minutes
Cooking time: 10 minutes

Ingredients:

8 eggs
1 tablespoon chopped parsley
200 g tinned tuna, with the
oil drained off
2 anchovy fillets
2 tablespoons olive oil
1/2 teaspoon salt, pepper

Cut the anchovies into fine strips. Lightly beat the eggs, add the anchovies and the flaked tuna. Season with parsley, salt and pepper.

Cook the omelette in the olive oil for 5 minutes each side. Serve at once.

Eggs baked in tomatoes
Œufs cocotte en tomate

Serves 6

Preparation: 1 1/2 hours
Cooking time: 30 minutes

Ingredients:

6 small eggs
6 large, firm tomatoes
40 g grated gruyère
1/2 tablespoon thyme
Olive oil
Salt, pepper

Wash the tomatoes. Remove one thick slice from the top and scoop out the flesh. Keep the flesh. Sprinkle the tomato shells with rough salt and turn them upside down on a plate to drain for an hour or two.

Cook the tomato flesh for 10 to 15 minutes on a high heat in 2 tablespoons of olive oil. Season with salt and thyme. Preheat the oven to 190°C (375°F, gas mark 5).

Place the tomato shells and their lids on an oiled dish and bake for 12 to 15 minutes. Remove from the oven and sprinkle with a little grated cheese.

Break an egg into each tomato shell, add the tomato purée and the rest of the gruyère.

Replace the lids and bake for a further 10 to 12 minutes. Serve the tomatoes as soon as they are cooked.

Piperade

Serves 6

Preparation: 40 minutes
Cooking time: 40 minutes

Ingredients:

1 kg tomatoes
4 red peppers
6 slices jambon de Bayonne
1 onion
1 clove garlic
Olive oil
6 eggs
Salt, pepper

Bake or grill the peppers first to make them easier to skin. Cut in pieces and remove seeds.

Plunge the tomatoes into boiling water for 30 seconds, skin and remove the seeds.

Slice the onion thinly and fry on a high heat in a little olive oil. Add the peppers. When they are almost cooked, add the tomatoes and crushed garlic. Season with salt and pepper and simmer gently until the mixture has turned to a purée.

In another pan, heat the ham for 1 minute each side and set aside where it will keep warm. Lightly beat the eggs. Remove the vegetable purée from the heat and stir in the eggs. Return to the heat and continue cooking gently, stirring continuously.

The mixture should remain creamy; do not let it dry up. Serve at once with the slices of ham.

Note:

If jambon de Bayonne is not readily available another raw dry-cured ham, such as coppa, prosciutto crudo or jamón serrano, may be substituted.

Baked eggs with anchovy
Œufs au miroir d'anchois

Serves 4

Preparation: 5 minutes
Cooking time: 4 minutes

Ingredients:

8 eggs
12 tablespoons tomato purée
A few leaves of tarragon and basil
4 anchovy fillets in oil
Pepper

Spread a layer of tomato purée in a shallow dish and sprinkle with tarragon and basil.

Break the eggs onto it, season with pepper and place in the oven at 190ºC (375ºF, gas mark 5) for 4 minutes.

Drain the anchovy fillets, cut them up and scatter over the eggs before serving.

Baked eggs with scampi
Œufs au miroir de langoustines

Serves 4

Preparation: 5 minutes
Cooking time: 4 minutes

Ingredients:

8 eggs
8 peeled scampi (Dublin Bay prawns, langoustines)
Chervil, chives
Parsley, tarragon
1 tablespoon olive oil
Salt

Chop the parsley, chives, tarragon and chervil. Cut the scampi tails across into slices and sprinkle with a little salt.

Fry for 1 minute in olive oil on a high heat, then add the chopped herbs. Place on a shallow ovenproof dish or in individual ramekins.

Break the eggs on top and complete cooking in the oven at 180°C (350°F, gas mark 4) for 3 to 4 minutes. Serve hot.

118

Eggs with poultry liver
Œufs sur le plat aux foies de volailles

Serves 4

Preparation: 10 minutes
Cooking time: 8 minutes

Ingredients:

4 eggs
4 chicken livers
40 g shallots, finely chopped
2 tablespoons olive oil
4 fresh button mushrooms
Salt, pepper

Fry the shallots in olive oil on a high heat for 2 minutes.

Slice the chicken livers and add to the shallots, over a gently heat so the livers remain soft.

Wash and slice the mushrooms and add to the pan.

Break the eggs top of all the ingredients in the pan and continue cooking until the egg whites are done.

Season with salt and pepper and serve immediately.

Minced beef in a cheese soufflé
Bœuf en soufflé

Serves 6

Preparation: 30 minutes
Cooking time: 20-25 minutes

Ingredients:

1 green pepper
2 onions
100 g fresh mushrooms
3 medium tomatoes
500 g minced beef
1 pinch oregano or thyme
2 tablespoons chopped fines herbes
Salt, pepper, Cayenne pepper
Olive oil

For the soufflé:

3 eggs
60 g grated cheddar
3 tablespoons low-fat crème fraîche
Salt, Cayenne pepper

Wash and chop the peppers into small pieces. Slice the onions thinly and fry with the peppers on a high heat in olive oil. Then add the mushrooms, washed and sliced.

Plunge the tomatoes into boiling water for 30 seconds, skin, remove the seeds and chop. Add to the pan, together with the minced meat, the fines herbes and the oregano. Season with salt, pepper and a dash of Cayenne.

Cook on a high heat, without a lid so that the liquid evaporates, then lower the heat and continue to simmer for a few minutes more.

Melt the cheese in a bain-marie and add the crème fraîche. Allow to cool slightly. Add the egg yolks and season with salt, pepper and Cayenne.

Beat the egg whites until they form stiff peaks and fold gently into the cheese mixture.

Spread the meat and vegetables in the bottom of a dish and pour the egg mixture over. Cook in a gentle oven (150°C, 300°F, gas mark 2) for 20 to 25 minutes.

Serve the soufflé as soon as it is cooked.

Lamb's heart kebabs
Brochettes de cœur

Serves 6

Preparation: 50 minutes
Cooking time: 20 minutes

Ingredients:

6 lambs' hearts
300 g smoked bacon
(in a piece not rashers)
250 g small onions
2 tablespoons olive oil
1 teaspoon thyme or oregano
Salt, pepper

Slice the hearts in half and soak in cold water for 20 minutes. Remove fat, trim away the tubes and cut into cubes.

Cut the bacon into chunks and blanch in boiling water for 5 to 8 minutes.

Place the bacon and the hearts in a terrine and leave for 30 minutes to marinate in the olive oil, flavoured with the thyme or oregano and seasoned with salt and pepper.

Peel the onions and plunge into boiling water for 30 minutes. Alternate pieces of heart, pieces of bacon and onions on the skewers and grill.

Ox tongue gratin
Gratin de langue de bœuf

Serves 6

Preparation: 30 minutes
Cooking time: 2 1/2 hours

Ingredients:

1 ox tongue (1.5 kg)
300 g thick tomato sauce
80 g grated Parmesan
5 tablespoons olive oil
1 onion
1 bouquet garni

Trim the tongue around the base and wash under cold water. Blanch in boiling water for 5 minutes and remove the scum from the surface. Drain, throwing away the cooking water. Make a court-bouillon, by adding the onion and bouquet garni to water, place the tongue in it and boil for 2 hours.

Remove from heat and allow to cool in the cooking liquid. Then skin the tongue and put aside until the next day.

Slice the tongue. Put some Parmesan in the bottom of a gratin dish and lay the slices of tongue on top. Add the tomato sauce and a little more Parmesan. Repeat the operation, finishing with Parmesan.

Place in an oven heated to 150°C (300°F, gas mark 2) until golden brown.

Parcels of calf's liver and mushrooms
Papillotes de foie de veau

Serves 4

Preparation: 10 minutes
Cooking time: 25 minutes

Ingredients:

4 slices calf's liver (120 g each)
4 shallots
1 tablespoon chopped parsley
200 g fresh button mushrooms
6 tablespoons olive oil
(or sunflower if preferred)
Salt, pepper

Wash the mushrooms and slice thinly. Peel the shallot and chop it. Mix the mushrooms with the shallot and chopped parsley and put through the blender.

Seal the slices of calf's liver in the olive or sunflower oil for 2 minutes each side. Season with salt and pepper.

Place each slice of liver on an individual sheet of kitchen foil and pile with the mushroom mixture. Close the foil to make parcels.

Cook in a moderate oven (180°C, 350°F, gas mark 4) for 15 minutes. Serve in the foil envelopes.

Lamb curry
Curry d'agneau à l'indienne

Serves 6

Preparation: 30 minutes
Cooking time: 1 1/2 hours

Ingredients:

1.5 kg shoulder of lamb with fat removed
3 good-sized onions
3 good-sized aubergines
1 pepper
1 tablespoon cumin seeds
1 tablespoon mustard seeds
2 1/2 tablespoons curry powder
Olive oil
Salt

Cut the meat into 3 cm pieces. Then, in a flameproof casserole, fry the chopped onions in olive oil over a low heat for 3 minutes.

Add the cumin and mustard seeds and stir for 2 minutes. Add the meat and brown, then salt lightly. Sprinkle on the curry powder, stirring it in.

Add 5 cl of hot water, cover and leave to simmer for just over an hour.

35 minutes into the cooking time, add the aubergines (chopped and with the skin left on) and the diced pepper.

Adjust the seasoning as necessary at the end of cooking. Add a drizzle of olive oil a few minutes before serving.

Lamb chops with mint
Côtes d'agneau à la menthe

Serves 4

Preparation: 20 minutes
Cooking time: 10 minutes

Ingredients:

8 lamb chops
1 tablespoon olive oil
Herbes de Provence
Salt, pepper
A few leaves mint

Brush the cutlets with olive oil and marinate for 15 to 20 minutes.

Mix the herbes de Provence with some of the mint, finely chopped.

Dip the cutlets in the herbs so they are completely coated. Cook under a hot grill and serve garnished with mint leaves.

Shoulder of lamb cooked in lemon
Epaule d'agneau au citron

Serves 6

Preparation: 15 minutes
Cooking time: 1 hour

Ingredients:

1 kg boned shoulder of lamb
4 tablespoons olive oil
2 medium onions
1 clove garlic
2 tablespoons paprika
2 tablespoons chopped parsley
3 tablespoons lemon juice
Lemon zest
Salt, pepper

Cut the lamb into 3 cm cubes and fry in a flameproof casserole, on a high heat in the olive oil. Once the meat is well browned, remove from the casserole and put on one side.

In the same casserole, fry the finely chopped onions and garlic. Add the paprika, chopped parsley, lemon juice and zest of lemon and then replace the meat in the casserole.

Season with salt and pepper, cover and simmer gently for 1 hour, adding a little water if necessary.

Serve hot.

Spiced veal with artichokes
Tagine de veau aux fonds d'artichauts

Serves 6

Preparation: 25 minutes
Cooking time: 1 hour 10 minutes

Ingredients:

1.5 kg lean shoulder of veal
8 cooked artichoke bottoms
4 large onions
4 tomatoes
2 lemons
2 cloves garlic
1 bunch parsley
1 tablespoon ground cumin
1/2 tablespoon turmeric
1 bay leaf
1 tablespoon ground ginger
1 glass dry white wine
1/2 glass virgin olive oil
Salt, pepper

Cut the meat into 3 cm cubes. Slice the onions and chop the garlic and parsley.

Place the meat in a dish with the garlic, parsley, onions and all the spices (cumin, turmeric and ginger) and half a glass of virgin olive oil. Season with salt and pepper and marinade for 20 minutes.

Remove the meat and fry in a flameproof casserole on medium heat. As soon as the meat is sealed, add the marinade and bay leaf and 25 cl of white wine.

Simmer gently for half an hour with the lid off. Cover and simmer for a further half hour. Meanwhile, cut the tomatoes and artichoke bases in quarters.

At the end of the cooking time, remove the meat from the casserole and set aside to keep warm. Add the tomatoes and artichoke bases to the cooking juices, together with the

Salad of avocados and artichoke bottoms with crab. p.108

Aubergines stuffed with tomato and mozzarella cheese, p.183.

Salad of mixed summer vegetables. p.82

Egg, tuna amd prawn salad with paprika dressing, p 84

juice of the 2 lemons. Cook on medium heat for 5 to 8 minutes.

Place the meat on a warmed serving dish, arranging the vegetables around it and spooning the cooking juices over.

Basque-style pot-roast veal
Veau à la basquaise

Serves 6

Preparation: 20 minutes
Cooking time: 45 minutes

Ingredients:

1.5 kg roasting veal
3 onions
3 aubergines
3 tomatoes
2 peppers
1 kg fresh button mushrooms
3 tablespoons olive oil
1 glass dry white wine
1 bouquet garni
1 clove garlic
1 lemon
Salt, pepper

Plunge the tomatoes into boiling water for 30 seconds, skin, remove the seeds and chop. Peel the aubergines and cut into cubes. Peel and slice the onions. Trim the mushrooms and wash well in water containing a little lemon juice.

In a flameproof casserole, fry the veal in the olive oil on a high heat, turning it to seal the meat on all sides. Add the onions and a little white wine, cover and cook for 25 minutes, turning the meat from time to time and basting with the cooking juices.

Add the tomatoes, aubergines, crushed garlic, sliced mushrooms, peppers (peeled and sliced) and the bouquet garni. Pour on the rest of the white wine, season with salt and pepper and simmer for a further 25 minutes.

Serve the roast veal surrounded by the vegetables and the gravy, removing the bouquet garni.

Veal chops with French bean and cheese topping
Côtes de veau gratinées aux haricots verts

Serves 6

Preparation: 10 minutes
Cooking time: 35 minutes

Ingredients:

6 veal chops (200 g each)
400 g frozen French beans
1 egg
3 tablespoons low-fat crème fraîche
3 tablespoons olive oil
50 g grated gruyère
Salt, pepper

Cook the French beans in water, drain and blend with the egg and the crème fraîche. Season with pepper.

Fry the veal chops in the olive oil on a high heat for 5 minutes each side. Season with salt and pepper.

Spread the French bean purée over the veal chops and sprinkle with grated gruyère.

Place in a hot oven (220°C, 425°F, gas mark 7) for 10 minutes until the cheese is browned. Serve at once.

Provençal beef casserole
Bœuf à la provençale

Serves 6

Preparation: 30 minutes
Cooking time: 2 hours

Ingredients:

1 kg beef (preferably chuck)
2 medium onions
1/2 clove garlic
4 tablespoons olive oil
1 kg ripe tomatoes
1/2 teaspoon thyme leaves
1/2 bay leaf
2 tablespoons chopped parsley
Salt, pepper, nutmeg
50 g black Nice olives
(or other black olives)

Peel the onions and slice thinly, and fry in olive oil on high heat.

Plunge the tomatoes into boiling water for 30 seconds, skin and remove the seeds. Add to the onions, along with the thyme, bay, garlic and chopped parsley.

Turn down the heat, cover and simmer. Add the meat, cut into 3 cm cubes and seasoned with salt, pepper and nutmeg. Pour on a little water if necessary.

Cook gently for 2 hours over very low heat. Serve decorated with black olives, added 10 minutes before the end of the cooking time.

Traditional beef stew
Pot-au-feu

Serves 6

Preparation: 30 minutes
Cooking time: 3 hours

Ingredients:

1 kg short rib with bone
600 g shin of beef
2 bones (e.g. rib)
without marrow
6 leeks
8 small turnips (navets)
2 heads celery
2 onions
2 cloves
Salt, 10 peppercorns
1 bouquet garni

Put the meat and bones in a large stockpot, cover with 4 litres of cold water and add a tablespoon of salt.

Bring to the boil and skim off the fat. Turn down the heat, cover and simmer for 1 hour.

Then peel the onions and spike with the cloves. Add to the stockpot, along with the bouquet garni.

One and a half hours into the cooking time, add the washed and prepared vegetables and 10 peppercorns. Add a little more water if necessary and simmer for a further hour and a half.

Cut the meat up and serve surrounded by the vegetables.

Suggestion:

Allow the stock to cool, degrease it and remove the bouquet garni, and use as a soup.

Marinated beef
Carpaccio de bœuf

Serves 6

Preparation: 15 minutes
Refrigeration: 2 hours

Ingredients:

800 g trimmed sirloin
1/4 litre olive oil
1 lemon, plus juice of 1 lemon
1 lettuce
Salt, pepper
Chopped parsley
Herbes de Provence, rosemary

Buy the meat trimmed of fat but not rolled and strung. Put it in the freezer for one hour to make it very firm.

Slice the meat extra-thin, using an electric or other very sharp knife, and lay the slices in a dish. Sprinkle with olive oil and lemon juice. Season with salt and pepper and the herbs and marinate for 1 hour in the refrigerator.

Serve 4 slices of meat per person, garnished with lettuce leaves, slices of lemon and chopped parsley.

This dish is eaten chilled, with the addition of basil or parmesan if liked.

Suggestion:

You could perhaps ask your butcher to slice the meat very thinly for you.

Fillet steak with creole sauce
Tournedos sauce créole

Serves 6

Preparation: 30 minutes
Cooking time: 40 minutes

Ingredients:

6 thick fillet steaks (150 g each)
1.5 kg tomatoes
3 shallots
4 cloves garlic
1 green pepper and 1 red pepper
2 tablespoons olive oil
1 bouquet garni
100 ml sherry vinegar
Salt, ground Cayenne pepper

Plunge the tomatoes into boiling water for 30 seconds and skin. Remove the seeds and chop. In a pan, fry the shallots and garlic in olive oil on a high heat. Add the tomatoes, the bouquet garni, a pinch of Cayenne and a little salt.

Cook uncovered until all the liquid has disappeared. Remove the bouquet garni and put the mixture through the blender.

Grill the peppers to make them easier to peel, and cut them up small. Add to the tomato sauce, together with the sherry vinegar, and cook for a further 5 minutes.

Grill the steaks and pour the sauce over them before serving.

Fillet steak with mushrooms
Tournedos aux champignons

Serves 4

Preparation: 10 minutes
Cooking time: 10 minutes

Ingredients:

4 thick fillet steaks (250 g each)
4 shallots
2 onions
500 g fresh button mushrooms
1 small sprig thyme
4 sprigs parsley
4 tablespoons olive oil
Salt, pepper

Chop the onions, shallots and parsley all together. Trim, wash and slice the mushrooms and cook for 5 to 8 minutes in olive oil on a high heat.

Then season with salt and pepper. Add the chopped onion mixture late in cooking.

Grill the steaks for 2 to 3 minutes each side. Season with salt and pepper.

Serve accompanied by the mushrooms.

Beef, pork and veal goulasch
Goulasch aux trois viandes

Serves 6

Preparation: 15 minutes
Cooking time: 2 1/2 hours

Ingredients:

300 g shoulder of veal
300 g shoulder or hand of pork
300 g braising beef
2 large onions
2 red peppers
3 tomatoes
3 tablespoons virgin olive oil
1 bouquet garni
2 tablespoons paprika
Salt, pepper, Cayenne pepper

Cut the meat up into small cubes (2 cm) and brown in olive oil in a large flameproof casserole. Remove from the casserole and keep warm.

Peel and slice the onions and fry them in the same casserole until golden, but without letting them go brown. Remove from the heat, return the meat to the casserole and sprinkle with paprika. Mix the ingredients well and put the casserole back over a very low heat.

Add water to cover the meat, and the bouquet garni. Cover and simmer for 1 hour.

Grill the peppers so as to peel them more easily. Cut into strips. Chop the tomatoes. Put the peppers and tomatoes in the casserole, season with salt, add a dash of Cayenne and simmer for a further hour.

Remove the lid, take out the bouquet garni and simmer further (not more than half an hour), until the sauce has thickened.

Serve piping hot.

Pork ragoût with cockles
Ragoût de porc aux coques

Serves 4

Preparation: 30 minutes
Cooking time: 1 hour

Ingredients:

800 g shoulder or hand of pork
1 litre cockles
6 tablespoons olive oil
4 cloves garlic
Juice of 1 lemon
1 tablespoon chopped parsley
Salt, pepper

For the marinade:

180 ml dry white wine
1 bay leaf
1 garlic clove
1 onion spiked with 1 clove
1 bouquet garni

Make a marinade with the white wine, the bay leaf, onion, salt, pepper and bouquet garni.

Cut the meat up, pour the marinade over it and leave it to marinate for a day. Wash the cockles very thoroughly, drain, open them up over a high heat and remove the shells.

Remove the meat from the marinade and dry on absorbent kitchen paper. In a flameproof casserole, brown the meat in olive oil on a high heat. Filter the marinade and remove the onion. Dry the onion on kitchen paper and slice, removing the clove. Add the onion and crushed garlic to the casserole to cook. Add the filtered marinade, cover and cook on low heat for 1 1/2 hours.

Check the casserole from time to time, adding a little water as necessary and turning the meat over. 5 minutes before the end of the cooking time, put the sauce through the blender and then add the cockles to it.

Add the lemon juice and chopped parsley to the sauce before serving.

Pork and leek ragoût
Ragoût de porc aux blancs de poireaux

Serves 6

Preparation: 20 minutes
Cooking time: 30 minutes

Ingredients:

1 kg boned shoulder or
hand of pork
2 kg leeks (white part only)
1 bunch thyme
1 sage leaf
2 cloves garlic
1 tablespoon olive oil
Salt, pepper

Trim and wash the leeks and cut into pieces. Blanch for 5 minutes in salted boiling water, and drain.

In a frying pan, brown the pork in olive oil. Remove the meat and discard the fat from the pan. Pour 200 ml of hot water into the pan and bring to the boil, scraping the cooking juices from the bottom so they are incorporated into the gravy. Pour the gravy into a casserole and replace the pork in it.

Add the leeks, the thyme, the sage leaf and the crushed garlic. Season with salt and pepper.

Cover and simmer for 30 minutes. Remove the bouquet garni (the thyme and sage leaf) before serving.

139

Jambon de Bayonne with spinach
Jambon de Bayonne aux épinards

Serves 6

Preparation: 15 minutes
Cooking time: 25 minutes

Ingredients:

6 generous slices jambon
de Bayonne (150 g each)
2 kg spinach
5 shallots
1 chicken stock cube dissolved
in 1/4 litre water
3 tablespoons olive oil
50 ml vinegar
1/2 chicken stock cube

Wash the spinach very thoroughly and cook in boiling salted water for 15 minutes. Drain.

Arrange the six slices of ham on a shallow ovenproof dish and surround with the spinach.

Place in a moderate oven (180°C, 350°F, gas mark 4), until the ham fat is translucent.

Fry the chopped shallots in olive oil until golden, add the vinegar and reduce.

Dissolve the chicken stock cube in hot water and add to the shallots. Reduce further for 15 minutes.

Pour this sauce over the ham and spinach before serving.

Rabbit with Mediterranean vegetables
Lapin niçois

Serves 6

Preparation: 20 minutes
Cooking time: 1 hour 20 minutes

Ingredients:

1 rabbit (1.5 kg)
4 onions
4 aubergines
2 green peppers
2 red peppers
5 courgettes
6 tomatoes
200 ml olive oil
1 bouquet garni
3 cloves garlic
Salt, pepper

Joint the rabbit and fry on high heat in 100 ml olive oil in a frying pan. Remove the rabbit pieces when they are browned and put on one side.

Slice the onions and peppers and, in a flameproof casserole, fry on a high heat in the remainder of the olive oil. When they are golden, remove and replace with the aubergines and courgettes, sliced into rounds. Then return the onions and peppers to the casserole, followed by the rabbit joints.

Plunge the tomatoes into boiling water for 30 seconds and skin. Remove the seeds and chop. Add to the casserole, along with the garlic, the bouquet garni and the salt and pepper.

Cover and simmer gently for 1 hour. Remove the bouquet garni and serve.

Rabbit with bacon and cabbage
Lapin aux choux

Serves 6

Preparation: 20 minutes
Cooking time: 1 1/2 hours

Ingredients:

1 rabbit (1.5 kg)
2 small new cabbages
250 g mild streaky bacon
(in a piece not rashers)
4 medium onions
30 g goose fat
or 300 ml olive oil

Dice the bacon and blanch in boiling water for 2 minutes. Drain on absorbent kitchen paper.

Wash the cabbages and cut in half to remove the core from the centre. Blanch in boiling salted water for 10 minutes, then drain.

Joint the rabbit and brown it on high heat in the olive oil or goose fat. When the rabbit pieces are well browned, remove and set on one side.

In the same pan, fry the diced bacon and sliced onions. Spread the cabbage over the base of a casserole and place the rabbit joints, the diced bacon and the onions on top.

Season with salt and pepper and add a 120 ml of water. Cover and simmer for 1 hour 15 minutes, adding a little more water as necessary.

Rabbit wrapped in bacon
Lapin enveloppé

Serves 6

Preparation: 25 minutes
Cooking time: 30-45 minutes

Ingredients:

1 ready-to-cook rabbit (1.5 kg)
12 thin rashers mild streaky
2 tablespoons olive oil
4 tomatoes
Thyme
Marjoram or rosemary
4 onions
Salt, pepper

Joint the rabbit, trying to make twelve pieces of more or less equal size. Season with salt and pepper, marjoram or rosemary and a small sprig of thyme.

Wrap a rasher of bacon around each piece of rabbit and arrange on a bed of sliced onion in an ovenproof dish.

Add the tomatoes, cut into quarters. Pour the olive oil over and place in a hot oven (200°C, 400°F, gas mark 6) until the juices run. Baste from time to time with the cooking juices as the rabbit cooks for 30 to 45 minutes.

Rabbit with green olives
Lapin aux olives vertes

Serves 6

Preparation: 20 minutes
Cooking time: 1 hour

Ingredients:

2 saddles of rabbit (800 g each)
200 g green olives
2 tablespoons tomato concentrate
3 cloves garlic
1 bouquet garni (thyme, rosemary, bay leaf)
2 onions
100 ml olive oil
400 ml white wine
2 sprigs fresh basil
Salt, pepper

Plunge the olives into unsalted boiling water for 1 to 2 minutes. Rinse in cold water, drain and remove the stones.

Joint the rabbit. In a flameproof casserole, brown the pieces in olive oil on a high heat, then remove and replace with the sliced onions. When these are golden, drain on absorbent kitchen paper. Discard the cooking fat and pour in the white wine.

Return the rabbit and onions to the casserole and add the tomato concentrate, half the olives, the peeled garlic cloves and the bouquet garni. Season with salt and pepper.

Cover and simmer for three quarters of an hour. Add the remainder of the olives 15 minutes from the end of the cooking time. Before serving, remove the bouquet garni and sprinkle with chopped basil leaves.

Ballotins of hare and chicken livers in a red wine sauce
Ballotins de lièvre

Serves 4

Preparation: 20 minutes
Cooking time: 25 minutes

Ingredients:

400 g boned hare
200 g chicken livers
2 eggs
Parsley, thyme
4 shallots
Salt, pepper

For the red wine sauce:

1/2 litre red wine
2 shallots
20 g butter
Salt, pepper

Fry the sliced shallots in a little olive oil over a high heat for 1 to 2 minutes.

Blend the meat with the chicken livers and season with salt and pepper. Add the egg yolks, one at a time, and the chopped parsley, thyme and shallots. Combine all the ingredients thoroughly.

Divide the mixture into four equal parts and wrap each in a piece of kitchen foil, in a fat sausage shape. Steam for 25 minutes in the pressure cooker.

Prepare the red wine sauce, as follows:

Reduce the red wine with the chopped onion, skimming off the surface from time to time to prevent bitterness. Add the butter and whisk. Season with salt and pepper.

Unwrap the "ballotins" and serve with the red wine sauce.

Suggestions:

The dish can be accompanied by, for example, cabbage, mushrooms or French beans.

Olives of turkey filled with ham and cheese
Cordon bleu en paupiette

Serves 4

Preparation: 10 minutes
Cooking time: 25 minutes

Ingredients:

4 turkey escalopes (100 g each)
4 slices smoked ham
150 g fontina (or similar) cheese
1/2 teaspoon herbes de Provence
1 tablespoon olive oil
Salt, pepper

For the sauce:

2 shallots
Olive oil
100 ml low-fat crème fraîche

Sprinkle herbes de Provence on the escalopes, place a slice of ham on each and spread the cheese on top.

Roll into an olive and secure with string. Season with salt and pepper. Cook, uncovered, in olive oil on a low heat for 20 minutes.

The olives can be served with a sauce made by frying the sliced shallots in olive oil and adding a little crème fraîche.

Sauteed turkey
Sauté de dinde

Serves 6

Preparation: 20 minutes
Cooking time: 50 minutes

Ingredients:

1.2 kg turkey breast fillets
4 large onions
6 tomatoes
3 red peppers
2 tablespoons sweet paprika
1 pinch Cayenne pepper
4 tablespoons olive oil
or goose fat
Salt, pepper

Plunge the tomatoes into boiling water for 30 seconds, skin and remove the seeds. Fry the chopped onions in 2 tablespoons olive oil. When they are golden, add the peppers, cut into strips, and the tomatoes.

Cook the mixture on low heat until it has turned into a purée. Season with salt, pepper, a pinch of Cayenne and the paprika.

Slice the turkey fillets, not too thinly, into escalopes. Fry on a high heat in 2 tablespoons olive oil or goose fat.

When they are just about cooked through but not too well done, turn down the heat and simmer for a few minutes more.

Serve right away with the vegetable puree.

Turkey with cep mushrooms and prunes
Dinde aux cèpes

Serves 6

Preparation: 30 minutes
Cooking time: 45 minutes

Ingredients:

600 g turkey breast
(in escalopes)
2 medium aubergines
500 g ceps
100 g prunes
1 tea bag
3 tablespoons olive oil
100 ml chicken stock
A few leaves tarragon
Salt, pepper

Stone the prunes. Make some weak tea and let the prunes marinate in it for 15 minutes.

Peel the aubergines and cut into large cubes. Cover with rough salt to draw out the liquid and leave for 10 minutes. Drain on kitchen paper and brown on a high heat in 2 tablespoons olive oil.

Rinse the ceps in lukewarm water, drain and chop into large cubes. Add to the aubergines and brown for a few minutes. Sprinkle with tarragon, season with salt and pepper, cover and simmer for 15 to 20 minutes.

Brown the turkey in 1 tablespoon of olive oil on a high heat, then add 3 tablespoons of chicken stock. Cook for 15 to 20 minutes, being careful to see the turkey does not dry out. At the end of this time, add the aubergines and ceps.

Cook the prunes for 5 minutes in a little olive oil and add them too. Serve right away.

Suggestions:

The ceps can be replaced by button mushrooms or, for a better flavour, by brown–capped (chestnut) mushrooms.

148

Braised duck with cabbage
Potée au canard

Serves 6

Preparation: 25 minutes
Cooking time: 2 hours

Ingredients:

1 duck (2 kg)
600 g mild streaky bacon
(in a piece not rashers)
1 strip fresh pork rind
(without fat)
2 small Savoy cabbages
1 tablespoon goose fat
Salt, pepper

Try to select two small cabbages and blanch whole in boiling water for 10 to 20 minutes.   Refresh under cold water, drain and remove the core.

Dice the bacon and blanch in unsalted boiling water for 5 minutes.   Drain on absorbent kitchen paper.

In a flameproof casserole, fry the diced bacon in goose fat on a low heat.   Place the pork rind in the casserole and add the cabbage leaves, salt and pepper and half a glass of water.

Cover and braise for 1 hour.   Check that the cabbage is soft and allow a little longer if necessary.

Brown the duck in a very hot oven (250°C, 500°, gas mark 9) for at least half an hour; it does not matter that it is not cooked through.   Joint it over a dish so that the juices are not wasted.   Season the joints with salt and pepper.

Add the duck joints to the cabbage, placing the thighs at the bottom of the casserole.   Pour the duck juices over and leave to cook for a further 20 to 35 minutes.

Duck breasts in green pepper sauce
Filets de canard sauce poivre vert

Serves 4

Preparation: 25 minutes
Cooking time: 20 minutes

Ingredients:

4 duck breasts
200 g mushrooms
1 lemon
100 ml red wine
1 onion
1 bay leaf
30 green peppercorns
1 tablespoon olive
or sunflower oil

Slice the onions and soften in 1 tablespoon olive (or sunflower) oil. Add the red wine. Leave on a high heat until the liquid has almost completely evaporated.

Add 1 glass of water, the bay leaf and green pepper and cook for 15 minutes.

Trim and wash the mushrooms and cook whole in water with the lemon juice for 5 minutes. Blend to a purée, season with salt and add the butter. Strain the sauce through a sieve and return to a low heat to reduce. Add the mushroom purée.

Cook the duck breasts in a non–stick frying pan with no added fat or oil. Allow 4 minutes each side on a medium heat.

The duck breasts can be sliced into long, thin strips. Serve covered with the sauce.

Duck with artichokes and olives
Canard à la provençale

Serves 4

Preparation: 25 minutes
Cooking time: 50 minutes

Ingredients:

1 oven-ready duck (1.2-1.5 kg)
4 skinned tomatoes
8 cooked artichoke bottoms
20 black olives
3 tablespoons olive oil
6 sliced shallots
1 250 g tin mushrooms
1 tablespoon low-fat crème fraîche
1 bay leaf, thyme, basil
Salt, pepper
1 clove garlic

Cut the tomatoes in quarters, remove the seeds and cut into strips. Cut the artichokes into thick slices. Stone the olives and slice in half.

Joint the duck and brown in olive oil on a high heat. Add the tomatoes, sliced shallots and garlic and season with salt and pepper. Blend the mushrooms to a purée and add a tablespoon of low-fat crème fraîche.

Add the mushroom purée, bay leaf and slices of artichoke.

Cover and cook over a medium heat for 50 minutes. 2 minutes from the end of the cooking time, add the black olives. Remove the bay leaf before serving.

Roast mallard with a puree of cep mushrooms
Canards sauvages rôtis et purée de cèpes

Serves 6

Preparation: 30 minutes
Cooking time: 30 minutes

Ingredients:

3 wild duck (mallard)
1 kg fresh or tinned ceps
500 g fresh button mushrooms
Salt, pepper
2 tablespoons low-fat crème fraîche

Clean the ducks and cut them in half lengthways. Roast in the oven at 200-220°C, (400-425°F, gas mark 6-7) for 30 minutes, basting frequently. Set aside to keep warm.

Wash the ceps, slice and cook on a low heat for 10 minutes in the cooking juices from the ducklings. Drain in a colander, purée and add the low-fat crème fraîche.

Wash and trim the button mushrooms and fry for 10 minutes. Serve the duck covered with the cep purée and accompanied by the button mushrooms.

Suggestion:

When wild duck is not available, the recipe also works well with normal duck or duckling. Brown-capped (chestnut) mushrooms can be used instead of ceps.

Poussins in lime sauce
Poussins aux citrons verts

Serves 6

Preparation: 45 minutes
Cooking time: 40 minutes

Ingredients:

6 375 gm poussins
6 limes
1/2 litre dry white wine
2 medium onions
2 tablespoons olive oil
50 g low-fat thick crème fraîche
Tarragon, parsley, basil,
chervil, chives, sage.
Salt, pepper

Marinade the poussins for 3 hours in the white wine, the juice of 4 limes, 1 tablespoon of olive oil, salt, pepper and all the herbs in equal quantities.

Fry the chopped onions in 1 tablespoon of olive oil on a high heat, adding a pinch of each of the herbs.

Spread the onion over the bottom of a roasting dish and arrange the poussins on top. Roast at 220°C (425°F, gas mark 7) for 25 to 30 minutes, turning occasionally.

Take two thirds of the marinade and reduce in a saucepan, skimming off the surface as necessary. When the poussins are cooked, remove the excess fat from the cooking juices and pour the marinade into the roasting dish, scraping the bottom of the dish with a spoon to incorporate the cooking juices.

Return to the casserole and simmer for a few minutes. Strain through a sieve. Add the crème fraîche and the flesh of 2 limes. Reheat but do not allow to boil.

Serve the poussins with the lime sauce poured over them.

153

Basque-style chicken
Poulet basquaise

Serves 6

Preparation: 30 minutes
Cooking time: 1 hour

Ingredients:

1 chicken (1.5 g)
2 large red peppers
2 large green peppers
4 medium tomatoes
6 medium onions
100 ml dry white wine
Olive oil
1 bouquet garni
Salt, pepper

Joint the chicken and fry on a high heat in olive oil.

When the chicken is golden brown, place in a flameproof casserole with the white wine, salt and pepper. Cover and simmer on a medium heat.

Grill or bake the peppers to make peeling them easier. Plunge the tomatoes into boiling water for 30 seconds, skin and remove the seeds.

Fry the sliced onions in olive oil on a high heat. Add the peppers, cut into strips, and the bouquet garni. After 10 minutes, add the tomato flesh.

Cook until a vegetable purée is obtained. Place the chicken in the purée, cover and simmer for 20 minutes. Remove the bouquet garni before serving.

Chicken and vegetable stew
Poule au pot

Serves 6 to 8

Preparation: 25 minutes
Cooking time: 1 1/2 to 2 hours

Ingredients:

1 oven-ready chicken (2 kg)
1 kg veal bones without marrow
2 heads celery
2 small turnips
4 small leeks
2 onions
1 bouquet garni
2 cloves
Salt, pepper

Place the veal bones and the chicken in a large stockpot. Cover completely with cold water and season with salt and pepper.   Bring to the boil and skim any scum from the surface.

Brown the peeled onions for a few minutes in a hot oven (220°C, 425°F, gas mark 7) and spike each with a clove.

Wash, peel and trim the vegetables (cut the celery heads in quarters) and add to the stockpot, along with the onions, the bouquet garni and a little salt.

When the liquid comes to the boil again, turn down the heat and simmer for 1 hours.

Serve the chicken surrounded by the vegetables.

Suggestions:

Remove the fat from the surface of the stock, which can then be strained and used as soup.   The chicken can be eaten with a special sauce, made from a small tin of button mushrooms, made into a purée, 1 full cream yogurt, 2 egg yolks, a little of the degreased stock, a dash of garlic, salt and pepper. Simply combine all these ingredients thoroughly.

155

Guinea-fowl with leeks
Pintade aux poireaux

Serves 6

Preparation: 15 minutes
Cooking time: 20 minutes

Ingredients:

2 guinea-fowl (1 kg each)
1 kg leeks (white part only)
300 ml chicken stock
2 tablespoons olive oil
Salt, pepper

Cut the whites of the leeks in half lengthways, wash and drain.

Cut the guinea-fowl in half lengthways and, in a flameproof casserole, brown in olive oil on a high heat for 5 minutes on each side. Season with salt and pepper, then add the sliced leeks and pour the hot chicken stock over.

Place, uncovered, in the oven at 220°C (425°F, gas mark 7) for 20 minutes. Remove the guinea-fowl from the casserole and keep warm. Reduce the cooking juices by half over a high heat.

Serve the guinea-fowl accompanied by the leeks, with the gravy poured over.

Chicken liver ramekins
Flans de foies de volailles

Serves 5

Preparation: 10 minutes
Cooking time: 25 minutes

Ingredients:

200 g chicken livers
5 eggs
3 shallots
2 tablespoons olive
(or sunflower) oil
20 ml Madeira or port
litre semi-skimmed milk
Salt, pepper

Fry the sliced shallots in olive (or sunflower) oil on a high heat.

Cut the chicken livers into small cubes. Remove the shallots from the heat and add the chicken livers to them.

Lightly beat the eggs and add to the chicken livers and shallots, along with the milk and Madeira. Season with salt and pepper.

Pour this mixture into five buttered ramekins and cook in a bain-marie in a slow oven (130°C, 250°F, gas mark) for 25 minutes.

Turn out and serve without delay.

Recommendation:

Half-way through cooking, cover with a sheet of kitchen foil to prevent the creams drying out.

Smoked haddock with yogurt sauce
Haddock sauce yaourt

Serves 4

Preparation: 10 minutes
Cooking time: 15 minutes

Ingredients:

4 pieces smoked haddock fillet
(150 g each)
1 litre semi-skimmed milk
1 bay leaf
For the sauce:
3 natural yogurts
100 ml low-fat crème fraîche
2 shallots
100 ml dry white wine
A few chopped chives
Zest of half a lemon
Pepper

Leave the smoked haddock to marinate in the milk with the bay leaf and pepper for 1 hour. Bring the milk to the boil and cook the fish in it for 7 to 8 minutes. Remove from the heat, and let the haddock cool in the milk.

Reduce the white wine with the sliced shallots on a high heat, until very little liquid remains. Add the crème fraîche and grated zest of lemon. Away from the heat, add the yogurts, whisking the mixture as you do so. Reheat the mixture without allowing it to boil.

Strain the sauce through a sieve and keep warm.

Drain the haddock fillets and serve with the yogurt sauce, decorated with chopped chives.

Hake with prawns and mushrooms
Cabillaud farci

Serves 4

Preparation: 35 minutes
Cooking time: 25 minutes

Ingredients:

1 kg hake (tail end or fillets)
400 g Greenland prawns
250 g fresh button mushrooms
Soy sauce
Chervil, coriander, parsley
240 ml dry white wine
1 kg courgettes
2 onions
Olive oil

Cut the hake in two to remove the central bone. Skin the fillets. Shell the prawns and put six to one side for decoration.

Trim and wash the mushrooms. Blend with the prawns, parsley, chervil and half the coriander. Add a little soy sauce. Spread this mixture on the hake fillets.

Cut the onions into rings and spread over the base of an ovenproof dish. Pour on 2 tablespoons olive oil and arrange the fish on top. Add the reserved prawns and the parsley. Pour the white wine over and cook in a hot oven (200°C, 400°F, gas mark 6) for 25 minutes.

Peel the courgettes, cut into thin rings and leave for 1 hour covered with coarse salt to draw out the water. Fry on a high heat in a little olive oil. When the courgettes are just soft, sprinkle with finely cut fresh coriander and season with salt and pepper.

Serve the fish accompanied by the courgettes.

Parcels of salmon fillet with a puree of green peppers
Filets de saumon en papillotes et purée de poivrons

Serves 4

Preparation: 15 minutes
Cooking time: 45 minutes

Ingredients:

4 salmon fillets (150 g each)
2 new onions
2 tablespoons low-fat crème fraîche
4-5 green peppers
1 lemon
5 tablespoons dry white wine
Salt, pepper

Wrap the peppers in cooking foil and bake in a hot oven (250°C, 500°F, gas mark 9) for 45 minutes.

Meanwhile, cook the sliced onions in the white wine until it has evaporated.

Season the fish with salt and pepper and squeeze a few drops of lemon over it. Wrap immediately in envelopes of cooking foil. Bake in a hot oven (250°, 500°F, gas mark 9) for 10 minutes.

Peel the peppers, cut them in half and blend with the onions and crème fraîche. Adjust the seasoning and serve the salmon surrounded by the purée of peppers.

Parcels of salmon steak with sorrel and mint
Darnes de saumon en papillotes à la menthe

Serves 6

Preparation: 15 minutes
Cooking time: 10 minutes

Ingredients:

6 salmon steaks (150 g each)
500 g tomatoes
300 g sorrel
1 bunch mint
100 g low-fat crème fraîche
Olive oil
Salt, pepper

Wash the tomatoes, plunge into boiling water for 30 seconds, skin and remove the seeds.   Chop.

Brush six pieces of cooking foil with olive oil and place a bed of tomato in each.

Place the salmon steaks on top, each with some chopped sorrel, 3 fresh mint leaves and a teaspoon of crème fraîche, and season with salt and pepper.   Close up the parcels and cook in a hot oven (220°C, 440°F, gas mark 7) for 12 minutes.

Kebabs of salmon and chicken liver with a cream sauce
Brochettes de saumon et foies de volailles

Serves 6

Preparation: 30 minutes
Cooking time: 10 minutes

Ingredients:

18 cubes fresh salmon
12 pieces chicken liver
2 chopped shallots
250 ml single cream
bottle dry white wine

Seal the chicken livers in olive oil for 3 or 4 minutes. On six skewers, alternate 3 salmon cubes and 2 pieces of chicken liver. Place, well separated, on an oven-proof dish and season with salt and pepper.

In a saucepan, reduce the white wine by half with the shallots on a high heat. Add the cream and simmer for 5 minutes.

Pour this sauce over the kebabs and place the dish in the oven at 150°C, (300°F, gas mark 2). Poach gently for 10 minutes. Remove the kebabs and keep warm.

Reduce the cooking sauce further to obtain a thicker consistency. Serve the kebabs hot, accompanied by the sauce.

Red mullet with Mediterranean vegetables
Rougets à la provençale

Serves 6

Preparation: 35 minutes
Cooking time: 15 minutes

Ingredients:

6 25 g red mullet (or 12 fillets)
300 g courgettes
300 g tomatoes
400 g aubergines
3 cloves garlic
1 teaspoon ground coriander
Thyme, bay leaf
Olive oil
1 lemon
Tarragon, chervil, parsley
8 leaves basil
Salt, pepper
Court-bouillon

Wash, scale and fillet the red mullet. Cook in a court-bouillon, uncovered, for 15 minutes. Remove from the court-bouillon and place in an ovenproof dish.

Strain the cooking liquid and pour a little over the fish so it is just covered. Cook in a hot oven (200°C, 400°F, gas mark 6) for 5 minutes.

Slice the tomatoes, courgettes and aubergines thinly and leave for half an hour covered with coarse salt to draw out the liquid. Arrange on a gratin dish and drizzle a little olive oil over.

Season with salt and pepper and add the sprig of thyme and the bay leaf, coriander and chopped garlic. Roast in a hot oven (200°C, gas mark 6) for 15 minutes. Remove the thyme and bay leaf.

Chop the basil, parsley, tarragon and chervil and mix with 6 tablespoons olive oil and the juice of a lemon. Season with salt and pepper and heat. Serve the red mullet fillets surrounded with the vegetables and with the dressing poured over.

163

Monkfish and bacon kebabs
Brochettes de lotte au lard

Serves 4

Preparation: 15 minutes
Cooking time: 15 minutes

Ingredients:

1 kg monkfish
16 thin rashers smoked bacon
16 fresh bay leaves
2 tomatoes
2 lemons
8 small onions
5 tablespoons olive oil
Salt, pepper
Parsley

Cut the monkfish into 16 pieces and roll each in a rasher of bacon.

Onto each skewer thread in turn a tomato quarter, 2 pieces of monkfish, 1 bay leaf, an onion and a lemon quarter. Repeat to complete the skewer.

Season with salt and pepper. Brush the kebabs with olive oil and grill for 15 minutes. Serve hot, decorated with chopped parsley.

Ballotins of fish served with cabbage
Ballotins de sandre au chou

Serves 4

Preparation: 25 minutes
Cooking time: 20 minutes

Ingredients:

500 g pike fillets
250 g fromage frais
4 egg whites
1 green cabbage
Salt, pepper

Blend the pike fillets and combine with the fromage frais. Beat the egg whites until they form stiff peaks and fold in gently to give a very smooth mixture. Season with salt and pepper.

Divide the mixture in four. Place each part on a piece of oiled cooking foil and roll up into a bundle. Cook for 10 minutes in the pressure cooker.

Wash the cabbage, remove the core and separate out the leaves. Season with salt and pepper and steam for 10 minutes.

Spread the cabbage leaves on a serving dish and place the ballotins of fish (removed from their foil wrappings) on top.

This dish may be served with a tomato coulis.

Poached mackerel with leeks in cream sauce
Maquereaux aux poireaux

Serves 4

Preparation: 30 minutes
Cooking time: 10 minutes

Ingredients:

4 mackerel (300 g each)
1/2 litre white wine
4 leeks (white parts only)
100 g low-fat crème fraîche
1 tablespoon chopped parsley
Olive oil
Salt, pepper

Clean the mackerel. Heat the white wine and poach the mackerel in it for 5 minutes.

Wash the leeks and slice thinly. Fry in 2 tablespoons olive oil, then add a little white wine, cover and simmer for 5 minutes.

Add the crème fraîche, salt and pepper just before removing from the heat. Serve the fish decorated with chopped parsley and garnished with leeks.

Fillets of sole with an aubergine puree
Filets de sole à la purée d'aubergines

Serves 4

Preparation: 20 minutes
Cooking time: 30 minutes

Ingredients:

4 sole fillets (150 g each)
1-2 ladles of court-bouillon
1 kg aubergines
1 lemon
100 ml olive oil
4 leaves basil
Salt, pepper

Grill the aubergines for 30 minutes, turning during this time, so that all the skin is well done (almost burnt).

Remove the skin and seeds and blend the flesh with the olive oil, lemon juice, basil, salt and pepper.

Arrange the sole fillets in an ovenproof dish. Pour the court-bouillon over and cook in a hot oven (200°C, 400°F, gas mark 6) for 5 to 7 minutes.

Arrange the sole fillets on a warmed serving dish with the aubergine purée around them.

Suggestions:

Spinach makes a suitable additional accompaniment.

Sole coated in grated Parmesan
Soles panées au parmesan

Serves 4

Preparation: 5 minutes
Cooking time: 10 minutes

Ingredients:

4 medium-sized soles
2 tablespoons olive oil
40 g grated parmesan
1 lemon
Pepper

Gut and skin the soles. Put the grated parmesan cheese and pepper on a plate, for the coating.

Roll the fish in the parmesan so it is completely coated.

Cook on medium heat in olive oil for 3 to 4 minutes each side. Serve at once with lemon juice.

Sole with a prawn and mushroom sauce
Sole normande

Serves 6

Preparation: 5 minutes
Cooking time: 20 minutes

Ingredients:

6 large sole fillets
Court-bouillon
100 g peeled prawns
1 125 g tin mushrooms
1 egg yolk
1 small pot low-fat crème fraîche
1 lemon
Salt, pepper

Prepare the court-bouillon and poach the sole fillets in it for 10 minutes, drain and put to one side where they will stay warm.

Mix together the prawns, the drained mushrooms, the crème fraîche and the lemon juice.

Place on a low heat for a few minutes. Remove from the heat and stir in the egg yolk. Season with salt and pepper.

Serve the sole accompanied by the sauce.

Grilled tuna with bacon
Thon grillé au lard

Serves 6

Preparation: 5 minutes
Cooking time: 30 minutes

Ingredients:

1 tuna fillet of 1.2 kg
12 thin rashers smoked bacon
1 tablespoon olive oil
Salt, pepper

Roll the tuna up in the bacon rashers and secure with string (rather like a giant tournedos).

Brush with olive oil on both sides and season with salt and pepper.

Cook under a hot grill for 15 minutes on each side. Serve at once.

Trout with melted cheese topping
Truite à la tomme de Savoie

Serves 4

Preparation: 15 minutes
Cooking time: 25 minutes

Ingredients:

4 trout (250-300 g each)
8 (5 mm thick) slices
tomme de Savoie or Emmental
1 small tin skinned tomatoes
500 ml olive oil
1 clove garlic
100 g onions
20 g basil
50 g parsley

Peel the garlic and onion and chop finely. Put the tomatoes through the blender. Fry the garlic, onion and tomatoes in olive oil on a high heat for a few minutes. Season with salt and pepper.

Clean the trout and place in an ovenproof dish. Pour the tomato sauce over, cover with a sheet of cooking foil and place in the oven at 200°C (400°F, gas mark 6) for 25 minutes.

10 minutes from the end of the cooking time, place two slices of cheese on top of each trout.

Serve decorated with chopped parsley and basil.

Turbot moulds with a watercress coulis
Flans de turbot au coulis de cresson

Serves 4

Preparation: 15 minutes
Cooking time: 1 hour 15 minutes

Ingredients:

500 g turbot fillets
8 scampi (Dublin Bay prawns, langoustines)
1 bunch watercress
200 ml single cream
500 ml low-fat thick crème fraîche
2 eggs
2 egg whites
1 bouquet garni
court-bouillon
Salt, pepper

Poach the fish in a court-bouillon with the bouquet garni and salt and pepper for 20 minutes. Drain. Cook the scampi for 2 minutes in boiling water, and shell.

Blend the turbot fillets, adding the eggs, lightly beaten. Add the thick crème fraîche and 500 ml of the court-bouillon, strained. Beat the egg whites until they form stiff peaks and fold them gently into the mixture to form a smooth mousse.

Butter 4 ramekins and place two scampi in the bottom of each. Pour in the turbot mixture. Place in a bain-marie and cover with a sheet of cooking foil. Cook in a gentle oven (150°C, 300°F, gas mark 2) for 20 minutes.

Wash the cress and blanch for 5 minutes in boiling water. Drain, put through the blender and strain.

Just before serving, add the single cream to the watercress purée and warm on a low heat, but do not allow to boil. Season with salt and pepper. Turn the turbot moulds out onto individual plates and serve with the watercress coulis.

Suggestion:

Brill can be used in this recipe in place of turbot.

Fish souffle
Soufflé au poisson

Serves 4

Preparation: 15 minutes
Cooking time: 40 minutes

Ingredients:

600 g haddock (or coley)
4 eggs
1 glass milk or single cream
Salt, pepper, nutmeg

Steam the fish for 6 to 8 minutes. Allow to cool, then flake and mix with the egg yolks, and the (warm) milk or single cream. Season with salt, pepper and nutmeg.

Beat the egg whites until they form stiff peaks and fold gently into the fish mixture.

Pour into a lightly buttered soufflé dish and place in an oven preheated to 210°C (420°F, gas mark 6-7) for 30 minutes.

Serve without delay.

Curried mussel stew
Mouclade au curry

Serves 6

Preparation: 20 minutes
Cooking time: 20 minutes

Ingredients:

2 litres mussels
50 ml olive oil
100 ml milk
100 g tinned mushrooms
3 shallots
4 egg yolks
1 teaspoon curry powder
1 lemon
1 bouquet garni
Salt, pepper
250 ml low-fat crème fraîche
120 ml dry white wine

Heat the white wine, with the bouquet garni, and add the mussels, on a high heat, so that they open. Remove the upper part of the shells. Place the mussels on a dish and leave in a warm place. Strain the cooking fluid and put on one side.

Slice the shallots and fry in olive oil, without allowing them to brown. Put the mushrooms through the food processor to purée them and add to the shallots. Stir, and then add the warmed milk, the cooking fluid and the egg yolks.

Season with salt and pepper, the curry powder and the lemon juice. Cook for 10 minutes, stirring continuously. Then stir in the crème fraîche. Pour the mixture over the mussels.

Place in a hot oven for 10 to 20 minutes. Serve at once.

Sauteed prawns with ratatouille
Gambas sautées et ratatouille

Serves 4

Preparation: 20 minutes
Cooking time: 20 minutes

Ingredients:

24 large prawns
1 aubergine
2 courgettes
2 tomatoes
1/2 red pepper
1/2 green pepper
1/2 yellow pepper
2 cloves garlic
3 sprigs parsley
Coriander seeds
3 tablespoons olive oil

Plunge the tomatoes into boiling water for 30 seconds, skin and remove the seeds. Seed the peppers and dice finely, but do not peel. Dice the aubergines and courgettes finely.

Using a non-stick pan, cover and sweat each type of vegetable separately for 10 minutes on a low heat.

Chop the garlic clove and the parsley. Put all the vegetables together in a skillet and fry on a high heat for 1 to 2 minutes in 2 tablespoons of olive oil.

Shell the raw prawns and remove the heads and tails. Heat 2 tablespoons of olive oil with the salt and fry on a high heat for 2 minutes.

Turn the prawns over and sprinkle with garlic and chopped parsley. Add the coriander and leave for one more minute.

Serve 5 or 6 prawns per plate with a little ratatouille.

Suggestion:

Frozen prawns are perfectly satisfactory for this recipe.

Greek-style scampi
Langoustines à la grecque

Serves 6 to 8

Preparation: 15 minutes
Cooking time: 40 minutes

Ingredients:

36 to 48 scampi (Dublin Bay
prawns, langoustines)
2 large tins skinned tomatoes
120 g feta cheese
2 chopped onions
1 large bunch parsley
200 ml dry white wine
2 tablespoons olive oil
1 teaspoon oregano
Salt, pepper

Shell the scampi, retaining only the tail. Rinse under running water and dry on kitchen paper.

Fry the chopped onions on a low heat in the olive oil. Add the tinned tomatoes, drained, the white wine, half the chopped parsley, the oregano and the salt and pepper.

Simmer, uncovered, until the liquid has evaporated. Place the scampi in a pan with the rest of the olive oil. When golden brown, drain.

Add to the tomatoes little by little and sprinkle with thinly sliced feta. Cook for 5 minutes, stirring very gently.

Serve decorated with chopped parsley.

ACCOMPANYING
VEGETABLES

Leek souffle
Soufflé aux poireaux

Serves 5

Preparation: 20 minutes
Cooking time: 35 minutes

Ingredients:

1 kg leeks (white parts)
500 g fromage frais
100 g grated emmental
150 ml low-fat crème fraîche
6 egg yolks
6 egg whites
Nutmeg
Olive oil
Salt, white pepper

Wash and trim the leeks and cut into slices. Blanch for 1 minute in boiling salted water. Drain well.

Mix the fromage frais with the crème fraîche. Add the egg yolks, then half the grated cheese. Season with salt, pepper and nutmeg. Beat the egg whites until they form stiff peaks, and fold into the mixture.

Oil a soufflé dish and pour in half the mixture. Add the leeks. Pour the remainder of the mixture on top and sprinkle with grated emmental.

Cover with a sheet of cooking foil and place in an oven preheated to 200°C (400°F, gas mark 6) for 20 minutes. Remove the foil and cook for a further 15 minutes.

Serve immediately.

Leek puree
Purée de poireaux

Serves 6

Preparation: 10 minutes
Cooking time: 25 minutes

Ingredients:

2 kg leeks
200 g low-fat crème fraîche
Juice of 1 lemon
Salt, pepper

Wash and trim the leeks and cut into slices. Cook in boiling salted water for about 20 minutes. Drain well.

Blend the leeks to a smooth purée and filter to remove the water.

Place on a low heat, add the lemon juice and season with salt and pepper. Whisk in the crème fraîche, so as to obtain a light mousse-like consistency.

Serve hot.

Suggestions:

This purée goes well with fish or white meat. Instead of leeks, it can be made with spinach, cauliflower, broccoli, courgettes, celery, turnips, mushrooms, pumpkin or green beans.

180

Mushrooms baked in a cream sauce with cheese topping
Gratinée de champignons

Serves 8

Preparation: 15 minutes
Cooking time: 20 minutes

Ingredients:

1.5 kg fresh button mushrooms
1 1/2 lemons
5 egg yolks
300 g low-fat crème fraîche
150 g grated gruyère
Olive oil
Salt, pepper
Nutmeg

Trim the mushrooms and wash under running water. Drain and dip in lemon juice to prevent discoloration. Slice thinly and fry on a low heat for 15 minutes in olive oil.

Mix the egg yolks and crème fraîche in a bowl, season with salt and pepper and add some grated nutmeg.

Spread the mushrooms in an oven-proof dish and pour the egg and cream mixture over.

Sprinkle with grated gruyère and place in the oven at 250°C (500°F, gas mark 9) to brown.

Serve at once.

Lettuce and sorrel mousseline
Mousseline de laitue à l'oseille

Serves 4

Preparation: 20 minutes
Cooking time: 30 minutes

Ingredients:

3 lettuce hearts
2 bunches sorrel
3 onions
150 g low-fat crème fraîche
1 tablespoon olive oil
Salt, pepper

Wash and spin the lettuce and sorrel. Remove the larger stalks from the sorrel leaves, and shred both lettuce and sorrel coarsely.

Slice the onions and fry for 5 minutes on a high heat in olive oil. Add the lettuce and sorrel, cover and cook on a low heat for 15 minutes.

Remove the lid and turn up the heat, so that any excess water can evaporate.

Just before serving, put through the food blender, add the crème fraîche and season with salt and pepper.

Suggestion:

This mousseline goes very well with fish or white meat.

Aubergines stuffed with tomato and mozzarella cheese
Aubergines farcies tomates et mozzarella

Serves 4

Preparation: 10 minutes
Cooking time: 40 minutes

Ingredients:

2 aubergines
2 tomatoes
200 g mozzarella
4 anchovy fillets
1/2 teaspoon oregano
Salt, pepper

Cut the aubergines in two and wrap in kitchen foil. Bake in a moderate oven (190°C, 375°F, gas mark 5) for 30 minutes.

Plunge the tomatoes into boiling water for 30 seconds, skin and remove the seeds. Dice the flesh.

Arrange the aubergines in an oven-proof dish. Fill them with the chopped tomato and season with salt and pepper. Cover with strips of mozzarella and an anchovy fillet.

Finally, add the oregano. Place in the oven at 250°C (500°F, gas mark 9) for 10 minutes until the cheese is melted and golden brown.

Serve at once.

183

Broccoli with slivered almonds
Brocolis aux amandes effilées

Serves 4

Preparation: 15 minutes
Cooking time: 15 minutes

Ingredients:

800 g broccoli
1 onion
30 g slivered almonds
3 tomatoes
Chopped parsley
Salt, pepper
2 tablespoons olive oil

Wash the broccoli and cook in boiling salted water for 10 minutes.

Plunge the tomatoes into boiling water for 30 seconds, skin and remove the seeds. Chop. Fry in olive oil in a saucepan, with the sliced onion and crushed garlic.

Add the slivered almonds, season with salt and pepper and cook for 15 minutes.

Drain the broccoli and serve with the almond sauce, decorated with chopped parsley.

Artichoke bases with mushrooms
Fonds d'artichauts aux champignons

Serves 4

Preparation: 15 minutes
Cooking time: 40 minutes

Ingredients:

8 artichoke bases
4 cloves garlic
2 lemons
250 g fresh mushrooms
Olive oil
Salt, pepper
Chopped parsley

Wash and trim mushrooms and slice thinly. Dip in lemon juice to prevent discoloration.

Fry for 10 minutes with 1 tablespoon of olive oil and the crushed garlic. Season with salt and pepper.

Steam the artichoke bases for 30 minutes (or 15 minutes in the pressure cooker). Pile the mushrooms on top and serve decorated with chopped parsley.

Artichokes and asparagus with cheese topping
Artichauts gratinés

Serves 6

Preparation: 10 minutes
Cooking time: 1 1/2 hours

Ingredients:

6 artichokes
1 onion
1/2 litre meat stock
1 small tin asparagus spears
120 g fromage frais
60 g grated emmental
Olive oil
Salt, pepper

Wash the artichokes and cook in boiling salted water for 20 minutes. Drain, trim and remove the hairy choke, retaining only the bases.

Fry the artichoke bases on a high heat for a few minutes in 3 tablespoons of olive oil, along with the sliced onion.

Add the meat stock, season with salt and pepper and cook for 30 minutes.

Drain the asparagus spears and fry for 5 minutes in 1 tablespoon of olive oil.

Arrange the artichoke bases in a gratin dish and add the asparagus spears. Spread the fromage frais on top and sprinkle with grated emmental.

Place under the grill for 10 minutes.

Serve without delay.

Suggestion:

Ready-to-use tinned artichoke bases are perfectly suitable for this recipe.

186

Courgettes with fromage frais stuffing
Courgettes farcies au fromage blanc

Serves 4

Preparation: 20 minutes
Cooking time: 40 minutes

Ingredients:

4 small courgettes
80 g low-fat fromage frais
2 egg whites
50 ml semi-skimmed milk
50 ml single cream
3 shallots
Olive oil
Salt, pepper, nutmeg

Wash the courgettes, slice in half longways and remove the seeds. Hollow them out slightly, saving a little of the flesh you scoop out. Blanch for 3 minutes in boiling salted water.

Fry the sliced shallots and the reserved courgette flesh in 2 tablespoons of olive oil, simmering on a low heat for 5 minutes.

Next add the milk and the cream, season with salt, pepper and nutmeg and simmer for a further 10 minutes. Remove from the heat and allow to cool slightly.

Beat the eggs whites until they form peaks and fold into the mixture, along with the fromage frais.

Stuff the courgettes with this mixture and place in a lightly oiled gratin dish. Drizzle a little olive oil over the courgettes to prevent them from drying out.

Bake in the oven at 200°C (400°F, gas mark 6) for 20 minutes.

Serve hot.

Tomatoes stuffed with mushrooms and fromage frais
Tomates farcies aux champignons

Serves 4

Preparation: 15 minutes
Cooking time: 20 minutes

Ingredients:

8 tomatoes
1 large tin button mushrooms
100 g very low fat fromage frais
Chives
Salt, pepper

Wash the tomatoes and cut a slice off the tops. Scoop out the flesh. Turn upside down to drain. Drain the mushrooms and purée them with the tomato flesh.

Add the fromage frais to the mixture. Season with salt and pepper and the chopped chives.

Stuff the tomatoes with this mixture and place in a hot oven (200°C, 400°F, gas mark 6) for 20 minutes.

Serve at once.

Suggestion:

This dish can also be made with aubergines.

Chicory in anchovy dressing
Endives aux anchois

Serves 4

Preparation: 10 minutes
Cooking time: 15 minutes

Ingredients:

8 small chicory heads
1 anchovy fillet
100 ml dry white wine
1 clove garlic
2 tablespoons tarragon vinegar
5 tablespoons olive oil
Salt, pepper

Trim off the base of the chicory. Fry the chicory heads on a medium heat for 5 minutes in 1 tablespoon of olive oil.

Add the white wine, salt and pepper, and braise for a further 10 minutes. Remove the chicory from the heat and set aside in a warm place.

Crush the garlic with the anchovy fillet. Combine with the vinegar, olive oil, pepper and 2 tablespoons of the cooking fluid from the chicory.

Serve the chicory with the sauce poured over it.

Celeriac and parmesan fritters
Céleris panés au parmesan

Serves 4

Preparation: 15 minutes
Cooking time: 10 minutes

Ingredients:

2 small roots celeriac
Juice of 1 lemon
4 egg yolks
250 ml low-fat crème fraîche
400 g grated parmesan
Olive oil
Salt, pepper, nutmeg

Peel the celeriac and cut across into large slices. Blanch in boiling salted water with a little lemon juice for 5 minutes. Drain and lay on absorbent kitchen paper.

Lightly beat the egg yolks and add the crème fraîche. Season with salt, pepper and nutmeg.

Dip the celeriac slices in this mixture and then into the grated parmesan.

Brown on a high heat in olive oil. Place on absorbent kitchen paper to drain the excess oil.

Serve hot.

Provençal vegetable mould
Flan de légumes à la provençale

Serves 4

Preparation: 15 minutes
Cooking time: 30 minutes

Ingredients:

500 g courgettes
4 eggs
2 red peppers
1 tomato
1 onion
100 g grated gruyère
4 tablespoons semi-skimmed milk
2 tablespoons olive oil
Salt, pepper

Wash and chop the courgettes without peeling. Wash and seed the peppers and dice them. Plunge the tomatoes into boiling water for 30 seconds, skin, remove the seeds and chop. Peel and slice the onion.

Fry all the vegetables on a high heat for 20 minutes in olive oil. Season with salt and pepper.

Lightly beat the eggs and add the milk and grated cheese. Season with salt and pepper.

Add all the vegetables, mix well and pour into a mould.

Cook in the oven in a bain-marie at 200°C (400°F, gas mark 6) for 30 minutes. Serve hot or cold with a tomato coulis.

Celeriac sautéed in goose fat
Céleris sautés à la graisse d'oie

Serves 4

Preparation: 15 minutes
Cooking time: 10 minutes

Ingredients:

2 small roots celeriac
Juice of 1 lemon
1 tablespoon goose fat

Peel and dice the celeriac. Blanch in boiling salted water, with the lemon juice added, for 5 minutes.

Drain well and place on absorbent kitchen paper. Then fry in the goose fat over a high heat until golden brown.

Place on absorbent kitchen paper to remove excess fat. Sprinkle with salt and serve hot.

Brown rice paëlla, p.235

Scallops served on a bed of leeks. p.228

Duck breasts in green pepper sauce p.150

Smoked haddock with yogurt sauce. p.158

Celeriac chips
Frites de céleris

Serves 4

Preparation: 15 minutes

Ingredients:

2 small roots celeriac
Juice of 1 lemon
Sunflower oil (for frying)

Peel the celeriac and cut into 'chips'. Blanch for 5 minutes in boiling salted water, with lemon juice added. Drain well and place on absorbent kitchen paper.

Fry in sunflower oil. When the celeriac chips are golden brown, drain and place on absorbent kitchen paper.

Sprinkle with salt and serve.

Suggestion:

These chips go well with any red meat.

CARBOHYDRATE DISHES

Broad beans with artichokes
Fèves aux artichauts

Serves 4

Preparation: 30 minutes
Cooking time: 30 minutes

Ingredients:

1.5 kg fresh broad beans
8 small artichokes
Juice of 2 lemons
15 shallots
1 sprig thyme
200 ml white wine
4 large tomatoes
Salt, pepper

Shell the beans and cook for 15 minutes in boiling water. Refresh with cold water. Split beans into halves and peel.

Trim the artichokes, retaining only the bases and dip in lemon juice to prevent discoloration.

Fry the sliced shallots on a high heat for a few minutes in a non-stick pan, with the juice of 1 lemon. Add the artichoke bases, thyme and white wine.

Season with salt and pepper, and simmer on a low heat for 15 minutes.

Plunge the tomatoes into boiling water for 30 seconds, so as to skin them more easily. Cut into quarters and remove the seeds.

Mix with the artichokes and the beans. Simmer, uncovered, for a few minutes, so that the liquid evaporates.

Split pea puree
Purée de pois cassés

Serves 4

Preparation: 12 hours 20 minutes
Cooking time: 1 hour

Ingredients:

300 g dried peas
1 onion spiked with 3 cloves
1 bay leaf
1 bouquet garni (1 sprig marjoram,
1 sprig thyme, 3 sprigs parsley)
50 g 'very low fat' fromage frais
Nutmeg
Coarse salt
Salt, pepper

Soak the split peas overnight in cold water. Then place in a pan with the coarse salt, onion and bouquet garni and cover with cold water.

Bring to the boil. Turn down the heat and simmer for 1 hour.

Drain the split peas, blend to a purée and strain. Add the fromage frais over very low heat. Do not allow to boil.

Season with nutmeg, salt and pepper.

Serve at once.

Lentils with tomato
Lentilles à la tomate

Serves 4

Preparation: 2 hours 15 minutes
Cooking time: 1 hour

Ingredients:

400 g green lentils
1 onion
1 tablespoon chopped parsley
1 clove garlic
200 g celery
Juice of 1 lemon
1 sprig thyme
6 tomatoes
Salt, pepper

Soak the lentils in cold water for 12 hours. Cook for 35 minutes in salted water, then drain.

Put the lemon juice in a non-stick pan, and fry the sliced onion, parsley, chopped garlic, celery (washed and cut into thin strips) and thyme. Season with salt and pepper and add to the lentils.

Plunge the tomatoes into boiling water for 30 seconds, so they are easier to skin. Cut in quarters and remove the seeds. Add to the mixture.

Place in a gratin dish and cook in the oven (130°C, 250°F, gas mark 1) for 20 minutes.

Serve right away.

Brown rice and aubergine bake
Riz intégral gratiné aux aubergines

Serves 4

Preparation: 20 minutes
Cooking time: 50 minutes

Ingredients:

200 g brown rice
2 aubergines
500 g tomatoes
2 onions
2 cloves garlic
Juice of 1 lemon
2 teaspoons thyme
100 ml meat stock
Salt, pepper

Cook the rice in boiling salted water for 35 to 40 minutes and drain. Wash the aubergines and cut into round slices. Leave for 20 minutes covered with coarse salt to draw out the water, then dry on absorbent kitchen paper.

In a non-stick pan fry the sliced onions and the crushed garlic for a few minutes in the lemon juice. Season with salt, pepper and thyme.

Separately, fry the aubergines and the chopped tomatoes in a covered non-stick pan.

In an ovenproof dish, arrange in turn a layer of rice, a layer of aubergines and a layer of tomato. Pour the meat stock over and place in the oven (190°C, 375°F, gas mark 5) for 30 minutes.

Serve hot.

Wholemeal spaghetti with courgettes
Spaghetti intégral aux courgettes

Serves 4

Preparation: 10 minutes
Cooking time: 10 minutes

Ingredients:

250 g 'very low fat' fromage frais
2 tablespoons chopped basil
2 teaspoons Dijon mustard
500 g courgettes
Juice of 1 lemon
400 g wholemeal spaghetti
Salt, pepper

Wash and dice the courgettes. Fry in a covered non-stick pan with the lemon juice until soft. Season with salt and pepper.

In a saucepan heat the fromage frais on a low heat, with the mustard and basil.

Cook the wholemeal spaghetti in boiling salted water for 3 minutes if fresh or 12 minutes if dried. Drain.

Serve the spaghetti on individual plates, arrange the courgettes around it and serve right away with the sauce.

Suggestions:

Spaghetti or, even better, tagliatelle can also be served with a sauce made from mushroom purée, 'very low fat' fromage frais, garlic, tarragon, salt and pepper.

PHASE II RECIPES

In the MONTIGNAC Method, Phase II follows naturally from Phase I; you are now, as it were, cruising.

It is in a sense just like Phase I, but with a wider margin of discretion. You need be less selective, which means that certain foods such as foie gras, scallops, chocolate and avocado can be reintroduced permanently.

Phase II is also the time when discrepancies become acceptable if they are carefully managed. But you need to make distinctions, for there are discrepancies and discrepancies. There are the very slight ones like salt pork with lentils, leg of lamb with flageolet beans, wholewheat pasta with bolognese sauce, or even bitter chocolate desserts. And then there are the serious discrepancies like steak and chips, paella with white rice or baba au rhum.

In this section we have included only the first kind of discrepancy, since the other kind belongs to a way of eating which is nutritionally bad. Even though discrepancies of the second variety may be tolerable within the context of a well-managed programme, they cannot actually be advocated, given the general principles of the Method.

STARTERS

Avocado bavarois
Bavarois à l'avocat

Serves 6

Preparation: 30 minutes
Cooking time: 10 minutes
Refrigeration: 6 hours

Ingredients:

6 avocados
2 tomatoes
2 lemons
7 egg yolks
3 leaves (1 sachet) gelatine
400 ml semi-skimmed milk
Salt, pepper

Plunge the tomatoes into boiling water for 30 seconds, skin, remove the seeds and chop. Cover with coarse salt and set aside for the liquid to drain off.

Make an egg custard as follows. Season the egg yolks with salt and pepper and beat. Bring the milk to the boil and add very gradually to the eggs, whisking vigorously all the time. Return to a very low heat and cook for 8 to 10 minutes, stirring until the mixture thickens. Remove from the heat and stir in the gelatine. If using leaves, first soften them in cold water and drain.

Cut open 3 avocados and remove the flesh. Sprinkle this with lemon juice and add to the custard. Add the chopped tomato, well drained. Chop the other 3 avocados, sprinkle with lemon juice and set aside.

Pour half the mixture into a loaf tin and allow to set in the refrigerator for 10 minutes. Remove from the refrigerator and arrange the reserved avocado flesh on top.

Cover with the remainder of the mixture and return to the refrigerator for 6 hours. Turn out and serve cold, maybe with a tomato coulis.

Cheese and walnut terrine
Terrine de fromage aux noix

Serves 4

Preparation: 15 minutes
Refrigeration: 6 hours

Ingredients:

150 g fromage frais
(well drained but not beaten)
100 g crème de gruyère (or similar
cheese)
150 g Roquefort
8-10 slices mozzarella
100 g shelled walnuts
2 tablespoons virgin olive oil
Salt, pepper, fresh basil

Blend the fromage frais and the crème de gruyère to a smooth, creamy consistency. Season with salt and pepper. Separately, mix the Roquefort with the olive oil.

Line a loaf tin with kitchen foil. Fill with, in turn, a layer of mozzarella (after which, season with salt and pepper, and sprinkle with basil), a layer of gruyère, a layer of Roquefort in olive oil and a layer of walnut pieces. Repeat until the tin is full.

Finish with a layer of mozzarella and a generous sprinkling of basil. Place a light weight on top of the terrine and refrigerate for at least 6 hours.

Turn out and serve well chilled.

Suggestion:

This terrine may be accompanied by a coulis made from fresh tomatoes with chervil, chives, parsley or basil.

Terrine of foie gras
Terrine de foie gras

Serves 5

Preparation: 10 minutes
Cooking time: 45 minutes

Ingredients:

1 kg fresh duck foie gras
100 ml pale port
Salt and pepper
Nutmeg

Place the liver in a bowl of iced water (the water should cover the liver completely) and leave in the refrigerator for 6 hours.

Trim and season with the port, salt, pepper and nutmeg. Place in a terrine dish and press well down so that it takes up the shape of the dish.

Cover with a sheet of kitchen foil and cook in a bain-marie in a slow oven (100/120°C, 200/230°F, gas mark) for 35 minutes.

Suggestion:

Armagnac or sauterne may be used instead of port.

Avocados with fromage frais
Avocats au fromage frais

Serves 6

Preparation: 20 minutes

Ingredients:

3 large ripe avocados
200 g fromage frais (not low fat)
1 full-fat natural yogurt
1 small clove garlic
1 small bunch parsley
1 small bunch chives
1 small bunch dill
2 egg whites
Lemon juice
Olive oil
Salt, pepper

Cut the avocados in half and remove the stones. Combine the yogurt with the fromage frais, the crushed garlic and the chopped herbs.

Season with a dash of lemon, a little olive oil, salt and pepper.

Beat the egg whites until stiff and fold gently into the mixture to obtain a mousse-like consistency.

Spoon this onto the avocados and serve chilled.

Tropical salad
Salade tropicale

Serves 6

Preparation: 15 minutes

Ingredients:

5 tomatoes
1 large tin hearts of palm
3 avocados
100 g black olives

For the vinaigrette:

1 tablespoon mustard
180 ml olive oil
40 ml sherry vinegar
1 lemon
Salt, pepper

Wash the tomatoes and cut into quarters. Cut the palm hearts across into fairly thick slices.

Peel the avocados, cut into pieces and dip in lemon juice to avoid discoloration.

Make the vinaigrette and season the tomato, palm hearts and avocado with it.

Serve chilled, garnished with black olives.

Foie gras with asparagus and artichoke salad
Salade au foie gras

Serves 6

Preparation: 40 minutes
Cooking time: 30 minutes

Ingredients:

500 g small fresh French beans
500 g green asparagus
2 raw artichoke bases
1 head frisée lettuce
6 slices foie gras (70 g each)
Lemon juice

For the vinaigrette:

6 tablespoons sunflower oil
2 tablespoons sherry vinegar
Salt, pepper

Dip the artichoke bases in lemon juice, cook in boiling water and cut into pieces.

Cook the French beans in salted boiling water, making sure they remain firm, and drain. Trim and cook the asparagus in the same way and drain. Allow all the vegetables to cool and mix them together. Wash and spin the salad.

Prepare a vinaigrette from 6 tablespoons of sunflower oil, 2 tablespoons of sherry vinegar, salt and pepper.

Pour the dressing over the vegetables. On each plate place two or three good-sized lettuce leaves, some of the vegetable salad and a slice of foie gras.

Serve at once.

Suggestion:

It is possible to use tinned artichoke bases, in which case they will not require cooking.

Scallops with an artichoke, pistachio and chestnut salad
Salade aux noix de Saint-Jacques

Serves 4

Preparation: 30 minutes

Ingredients:

1 head frisée lettuce
1 batavia lettuce
50 g dried pistachios
4 cooked artichoke bases
350 g scallops,
cooked and shelled
200 g chestnuts in water
250 g vinaigrette (olive oil and vinegar)
Tarragon, chives
Salt, pepper

Wash and spin the lettuces. Chop the pistachios and add them to the vinaigrette. Cut the artichoke bases into strips and dip them in the vinaigrette.

Slice the scallops, season with salt, pepper and the vinaigrette and marinade for 15 minutes.

Mix the lettuce with the vinaigrette and the finely chopped chestnuts. Arrange the scallops on top and decorate with the artichoke, tarragon and chopped chives.

Scallops served with sauerkraut and asparagus
Salade de choucroute et noix de Saint-Jacques

Serves 4

Preparation: 10 minutes
Cooking time: 7 minutes

Ingredients:

600 g raw sauerkraut
12 asparagus tips
8 raw scallops
Juice of 1 lemon
3 tablespoons olive oil
Chervil, salt, pepper

Marinade the sauerkraut in the lemon juice, salt, pepper and olive oil. Steam the asparagus tips for 7 minutes or cook in salted boiling water for 5 minutes.

Cut each of the scallops in half. Cook in a frying-pan over a high heat for 1 minute each side. Season with salt and pepper.

Place the sauerkraut on individual plates and arrange the scallops and asparagus on top.

To serve, decorate with chervil.

Smoked haddock with green lentils
Salade de lentilles au haddock

Serves 4

Preparation: 20 minutes
Cooking time: 30 minutes

Ingredients:

200 g green lentils
250 g fresh smoked haddock
1 onion, 1 bouquet garni
1 clove
1/4 litre semi-skimmed milk
Salt, peppercorns

For the dressing:

4 tablespoons olive oil
1 tablespoon balsamic vinegar
1 teaspoon mustard
Salt, pepper, parsley or chives

Soak the lentils for 12 hours. Peel the onion and spike it with the clove. Place the bouquet garni and onion in a casserole, add the lentils and cold water to cover.

Bring to the boil and simmer for 30 minutes. Season with salt after cooking.

Soak the haddock in the milk for 6 hours to draw out the water. Drain. Bring the milk to the boil, add the haddock and cook for 7 to 8 minutes.

Make a vinaigrette from the olive oil, vinegar, mustard and seasonings. Drain the lentils. Cut the fish into pieces, mingle all the ingredients together and serve.

Salad of haricot beans and mussels
Salade de haricots blancs et moules

Serves 6

Preparation: 25 minutes
Cooking time: 1 hour

Ingredients:

1 bowl dried haricot beans
1.5 litres mussels
2 tomatoes
2 onions
2 small onions
1 bouquet garni
1 tablespoon chopped parsley
1 tablespoon vinegar
1 teaspoon mustard
1 tablespoon low-fat crème fraîche
Salt, pepper

Soak the beans in water for 12 hours. Cook for 1 hour in salted water, with the two onions and the bouquet garni. Drain and allow to cool.

Wash the mussels, place them over a high heat to open up, and remove the shells. Make a vinaigrette and add the crème fraîche, the small onions, chopped, and the parsley. Season with salt and pepper.

Before serving, mix together the mussels and the beans in the dressing and allow to stand for a while. Decorate with slices of tomato.

Salade niçoise with wholegrain rice
Salade niçoise de riz intégral

Serves 6-8

Preparation: 10 minutes
Cooking time: 15 to 18 minutes
Refrigeration: 30 minutes

Ingredients:

400 g long wholegrain rice
1 cucumber
1 green and 1 red pepper
6 firm tomatoes
125 g black olives
2 fresh white onions
1 clove garlic
1 small tin anchovies in oil
2 small tins tuna in oil

For the dressing:

4 tablespoons olive oil
1 tablespoon vinegar
1 teaspoon mustard
Salt, pepper

Cook the rice in salted boiling water for 35 to 40 minutes. Rinse and drain.

Peel the cucumber. Dice the cucumber, tomatoes and peppers. Mix with the chopped onions and the flaked tuna.

Make a vinaigrette dressing and add to the salad ingredients. Mix thoroughly with the rice and allow to stand in the refrigerator for 30 minutes.

Serve chilled.

Wholemeal taboulé
Taboulé intégral

Serves 6

Preparation: 2 1/2 hours

Ingredients:

200 g wholemeal semolina
500 g tomatoes
1/2 cucumber
12 small onions
2 lemons
2 tablespoons chopped parsley
1 tablespoon chopped fresh mint
6 tablespoons olive oil
Salt, pepper

Peel and dice the cucumber. Peel and chop the tomatoes, but do not drain, as they need to conserve all their juice.

Mix the cucumber and tomatoes with the semolina, parsley, chopped mint, lemon juice and olive oil. Season with salt and pepper. Leave in the refrigerator for at least 6 hours for the semolina to swell. Stir occasionally.

Serve chilled, decorated with the little onions and mint leaves.

Wholemeal gnocchi
served with a tomato and basil coulis
Gnocchi intégral au basilic

Serves 6

Preparation: 1 1/2 hours
Cooking time: 15 minutes

Ingredients:

1 litre semi-skimmed milk
300 g wholemeal semolina
3 egg yolks
3 tablespoons olive oil
100 g grated gruyère
Salt, pepper, nutmeg
Basil

Bring the milk to the boil and sprinkle the semolina into it. Cook on a low heat for 10 minutes, stirring continuously, until the mixture is thick.

Season with salt, pepper, nutmeg and olive oil. Remove from the heat. Add the egg yolks one at a time, mixing well to form a dough.

Moisten a large sheet of kitchen foil. Roll out the dough onto it, to a thickness of half a centimetre. Leave to cool.

Cut out the gnocchi to your chosen shape. Place in a gratin dish, sprinkle with grated gruyère and drizzle a little olive oil over.

Place in a hot oven (250°C, 500°F, gas mark 9) for 15 minutes.

Make a tomato and basil coulis (see recipe on page 77).

Serve hot, accompanied by the coulis.

THE MAIN COURSE

Quails' eggs with scallops
Œufs de caille
aux noix de Saint-Jacques

Serves 4

Preparation: 10 minutes
Cooking time: 5 minutes

Ingredients:

8 quail's eggs
4 raw scallops
20 g single cream
4 tablespoons white wine
Chives and chopped parsley
Salt, pepper
4 empty scallop shells

Cut each scallop into three and arrange on the shells with a tablespoon of white wine per shell.

Season with salt and pepper. Into each shell break 2 quail's eggs. Cover with single cream.

Cook in an oven set at 220°C (425°F, gas mark 7) for 5 minutes.

To serve, decorate with chives and chopped parsley.

Goose foie gras with scallops
Foie gras d'oie aux Saint-Jacques

Serves 6

Preparation: 1 hour
Cooking time: 30 minutes

Ingredients:

1 fresh 800 g foie gras
8 good-sized scallops
1/2 glass port
Salt, sweet paprika

Clean the scallops and open them by placing over a high heat for a few seconds. Separate the white parts from the corals (roes) and slice the whites thinly. Season with salt and sweet paprika. Blend the corals to a purée with the port and some sweet paprika.

Place the foie gras in iced water for 6 hours. Trim and season with salt and pepper.

Place some of the scallop in the bottom of a terrine dish and lay the foie gras on top. Press down well so that it takes up the shape of the dish. Pour the coral purée over and cover with the remaining scallop slices.

Cover with a sheet of kitchen foil and cook in a bain-marie in a slow oven (100/120°C, 200/230°, gas mark 1/4) for 35 minutes.

Serve lukewarm.

Suggestion:

Duck foie gras can be served in the same way.

Scallops with raw ham
Noix de Saint-Jacques au jambon

Serves 4

Preparation: 10 minutes
Cooking time: 25 minutes

Ingredients:

16 raw scallops
1 tablespoon olive oil
1 shallot
150 g raw ham
4 tablespoons low-fat crème fraîche
1 glass dry white wine
Salt, pepper

Fry the chopped shallot in the olive oil. Add the scallops and fry for a further 2 minutes only. Season with salt and pepper.

Add the white wine and the ham, cut into broad strips. Simmer on a low heat for 15 minutes.

Add the crème fraîche just before serving.

Scallops served on a bed of leeks
Saint-Jacques sur lit de poireaux

Serves 4

Preparation: 10 minutes
Cooking time: 15 minutes

Ingredients:

16 scallops
200 g leeks (white part only)
8 tablespoons olive oil
1 glass dry white wine
A few leaves tarragon

Clean the leeks and slice thinly. Fry on a low heat in 2 tablespoons olive oil, without browning. Add the white wine and simmer for 15 minutes.

In another pan, sauté the scallops in olive oil for 2 minutes each side. Season with salt, pepper and chopped tarragon.

Place the leeks on warmed individual plates. Arrange the scallops on top. Season with pepper, and serve.

Oysters
and mushrooms in mushroom sauce
Champignons de Paris aux huîtres

Serves 6

Preparation: 15 minutes
Cooking time: 20 minutes

Ingredients:

36 fresh button mushrooms
36 oysters (preferably Mareenes or Oléron types)
1/2 litre whipped cream
2 egg yolks
1/2 glass armagnac

Trim and wash the mushrooms and dry with a cloth. Separate the caps from the stems.

Open the oysters and remove from their shells. Filter the liquid which comes out and reserve. Put the mushroom tails stems the blender, adding a little of the oyster liquid to obtain a fine purée consistency.

On a low heat, fry the mushroom caps in a little oil for 15 minutes.

When cooked, remove from the pan and set aside to keep warm.

Degrease the pan and pour in the armagnac, the oysters and half the liquid from them. Bring to the boil for 30 seconds and remove the oysters. Keep warm.

Pour the mushroom purée into the pan and reduce to make a thick sauce.

Mix the whipped cream with the two egg yolks and add to the reduced mushroom purée.

Serve the mushrooms with the oysters, with the sauce poured over.

Oysters served hot with raw ham
Huîtres chaudes au jambon

Serves 4

Preparation: 10 minutes
Cooking time: 18 minutes

Ingredients:

4 dozen good-sized oysters
2 good-sized slices raw ham
2 shallots, finely chopped
200 g fresh mushrooms, sliced
1 tablespoon lemon juice
2 pinches celery salt
100 ml low-fat crème fraîche
2 tablespoons chopped parsley
Salt, pepper

Open the oysters and remove from the shells. Filter the liquid. Cut the ham into strips and fry on a high heat.

Add the liquid from the oysters, together with the shallots, the sliced mushrooms, lemon juice, salt, pepper and celery salt. Simmer, covered, for 5 minutes. Uncover and simmer for a further 5 minutes to reduce the cooking liquid.

Add the oysters and bring to the boil. Finally stir in the cream, sprinkle with parsley and leave over the heat for a further minute, stirring all the time.

Serve at once on warmed plates.

Oyster omelette
Omelette aux huîtres

Serves 4

Preparation: 15 minutes
Cooking time: 7 minutes

Ingredients:

8 eggs
12 oysters (flat Belon type)
2 tablespoons chopped flat-leaved parsley
A dash of saffron
2 tablespoons single cream
Salt, pepper
3 tablespoons sunflower oil

Open the oysters and remove from their shells. Keep the liquid and filter it into a saucepan. Heat the liquid but do not allow to boil. Plunge the oysters in for 30 seconds. Remove and set aside to keep warm.

Lightly beat the eggs with 2 tablespoons of the cooking liquid, a dash of saffron, salt and pepper.

Cook the omelette in sunflower oil. When it is almost ready, place the oysters (drained on absorbent kitchen paper) in the centre.

Fold the omelette and serve right away.

Oysters in a sabayon
Huîtres en sabayon

Serves 4

Preparation: 20 minutes
Cooking time: 5 minutes

Ingredients:

24 oysters (preferably from Mareenes or Oléron
6 egg yolks
400 g tomatoes
1 lemon
1 tablespoon finely chopped chives
3 tablespoons low-fat cream
Coarse salt, pepper

Open the oysters and detach from their shells, but leave in the shells. Collect 150 ml of the liquid and filter it.

Plunge the tomatoes into boiling water for 30 seconds, skin and remove the seeds. Dice the flesh and leave to drain in a colander.

In a bain-marie, gently heat the egg yolks and the liquid from the oysters, whisking with an electric hand-whisk. Turn the heat up as the mixture begins to froth up. Season the whipped mixture with the pepper and chives. Add the whipped cream and a few drops of lemon juice.

Preheat the grill. Divide the diced tomato among the oysters and spoon the sabayon mixture on top.

Place the sea salt in an ovenproof dish to make a bed on which the oysters can be placed. Grill for 1 minute. Serve immediately.

Liver and bacon
Poêlée de foie de génisse

Serves 4

Preparation: 20 minutes
Cooking time: 10 minutes

Ingredients:

8 slices of ox or calf liver
(80 g each)
400 g onions
200 g thin rashers lean bacon
1 pinch thyme
Salt, pepper

Peel and finely chop the onions. Fry the bacon rashers and keep them warm. Then, in the same pan, sweat the onion on a low heat.

Add the slices of liver and cook for 2 to 3 minutes each side. Season with salt, pepper and thyme. Arrange on individual plates on a bed of onion.

Serve with the bacon rashers placed on top.

Chili con carne

Serves 6

Preparation: 30 minutes
Cooking time: 3 hours

Ingredients:

1 kg minced beef
300 g red kidney beans
3 onions
1 green pepper
2 cloves garlic
1 kg tinned tomatoes
100 ml olive oil
2 Cayenne (finger) peppers
1 teaspoon ground cumin
litre chicken stock
1 teaspoon paprika

Soak the red kidney beans in cold water for 12 hours. Drain, cover with cold water, bring to the boil and cook on a medium heat for 1 hours. Half-way through cooking, add salt and skim. When the beans are done, drain and set on one side.

On a high heat, fry the minced beef in a flame-proof casserole in 3 tablespoons olive oil. Season with salt and paprika. Simmer for 10 minutes. Remove the meat and set on one side.

Wash and dice the green pepper and fry on a low heat in the casserole in 2 tablespoons olive oil. Add the sliced onions and the crushed garlic. When the onions are translucent, add the Cayenne peppers and the cumin.

Return the meat to the casserole and pour in the chicken stock. Add the tomatoes and mingle the ingredients together. Cover and cook on a low heat for 40 minutes. Then add the red kidney beans and replace over a low heat to cook, uncovered, for a further 30 minutes.

Add more stock during cooking if necessary.

Serve hot.

Brown rice paëlla
Paëlla au riz intégral

Serves 6

Preparation: 1 hour
Cooking time: 1 hour

Ingredients:

1 large chicken (1.2 kg), jointed
and with all fat removed
500 g squid
500 g scampi
A dozen large mussels
350 g long-grain brown rice
250 g peas
750 g tinned peeled tomatoes
3 good-sized onions
4-5 tablespoons olive oil
1 good pinch saffron
Salt, pepper

Soak the brown rice in cold water for 3 hours. Drain and part-cook for 15 minutes. In a large pan or paëlla dish, fry the chicken joints in olive oil until they are golden. Remove and set aside.

In the same pan, fry the chopped onions. Add the tomatoes, chopped and drained. Return the chicken to the pan, season with salt and pepper and mingle the ingredients thoroughly. Simmer for 30 minutes, adding a little boiling water if necessary.

Add the squid, cleaned and sliced in rings, together with the peas and the scampi. Strew the partly cooked rice into the pan, which should at this stage contain at least 750 ml of liquid.

Cook for 10 minutes, stirring continuously. Sprinkle with saffron and cook for a further 25 minutes, continuing to stir.

Wash the mussels, scraping them well, and add them 5 minutes from the end of the cooking time, so that they open up.

235

Couscous made with wholemeal semolina
Couscous intégral

Serves 8

Preparation: 1 hour 20 minutes
Cooking time: 1 hour 10 minutes

Ingredients:

1 kg wholemeal semolina
1 kg lamb (neck, breast, shoulder)
1 chicken (1.2 kg), jointed
4 small turnips
4 courgettes
1 piece marrow
250 g tinned chick-peas
500 g onions
1 pepper
200 g raisins
2 tomatoes
1 tablespoon Moroccan ground cumin
1 pinch ground cinnamon
1 tablespoon ras el hanout (harissa)
1 tablespoon olive oil

Rinse the semolina in cold water in a sieve, then add a little salt and leave it to swell up for half an hour, stirring regularly. Use a large shallow dish for this, spreading it evenly to avoid bubbles forming.

Boil the water in a couscoussier (or a suitable steamer). As soon as it is steaming, place the semolina over the steam and cook for 15 minutes.

Remove the semolina, pour a glass of water over it and leave it on a large dish to swell again for 15 minutes. When it has cooled, return it to the couscoussier and steam for a further 15 minutes. While still hot, pour on a little olive oil and mix in well.

Empty the water out of the couscoussier. In a pan, fry the lamb on a high heat in olive oil. Set aside and repeat the procedure with the chicken.

In the same pan, fry the sliced onions and the quartered tomatoes. Return the lamb to the pan. Season with the cumin, cinnamon, ras el hanout and salt.

Place the lamb, onions and tomatoes in the couscoussier, add 1 litres of boiling water and cook on a low heat for 30 minutes. Add the chicken and vegetables (washed and cut into pieces); begin with the courgettes, adding the pepper and marrow 15 minutes later. Cook for 40 minutes. 15 minutes before the end of cooking time, add the chick-peas.

Serve the semolina separately in a large dish. The raisins, after standing in lukewarm water to swell for a few hours, are drained and are also served separately.

Recommendation:

The semolina can equally be steamed over the meat and vegetables, when it will absorb some of the flavours.

Blanquette of veal with brown rice
Blanquette de veau au riz intégral

Serves 6

Preparation: 20 minutes
Cooking time: 2 hours 15 minutes

Ingredients:

1.2 kg veal pieces (shoulder, breast, thick flank)
1 onion spiked with a clove and a bay leaf
1 bouquet garni
100 g mushroom purée (see recipe page 151)
40 ml dry white wine
2 egg yolks
200 ml low-fat crème fraîche
1 tablespoon lemon juice
Cayenne pepper or nutmeg
Salt, white pepper

Blanch the meat in 750 ml of boiling water, with the spiked onion, the bouquet garni, salt and pepper. Skim and simmer for 2 hours.

Drain off the meat, remove the bouquet garni and strain the cooking fluid through a sieve. Dilute the mushroom purée with the cooking fluid and bring to the boil.

Place in a casserole with the meat, add the white wine and simmer on a low heat for a further 15 minutes.

Cook the brown rice in boiling salted water for 35 to 40 minutes. Drain.

Beat the egg yolks with the crème fraîche and pour into the casserole, a little at a time. Stir thoroughly and season with the lemon juice and Cayenne pepper (or nutmeg).

Serve the veal with the brown rice and the sauce.

Cassoulet from the Gers region of South West France
Cassoulet gersois

Serves 6 to 8

Preparation: 20 minutes
Cooking time: 2 1/2 to 3 hours

Ingredients:

500 g good quality dried haricot beans
6 to 8 joints goose confit
1 tin gésiers confits (gizzards)
1 tin stuffed goose neck
2 onions
2 or 3 tomatoes
3 cloves garlic
2 bouquets garnis
Salt, pepper

Soak the beans in water for 12 hours. Drain, place in unsalted cold water and cook for 1 hour, adding salt and a bouquet garni half-way through cooking. Reserve the cooking water.

In a flame-proof casserole, fry the chopped onions in goose fat over a medium heat. Plunge the tomatoes into boiling water for 30 seconds, skin, remove the seeds and chop. Add to the onions, together with the crushed garlic cloves and the second bouquet garni.

Separate out the duck confit joints and draw out the fat by placing them in the oven for 2 or 3 minutes at 70°C (200°F or the lowest gas mark possible). Retain 2 tablespoons of this fat and add to the casserole. Remove the fat from the gizzards, cut them in strips and sear them in a pan for a few moments in a tablespoon of their fat. Do the same with the stuffed goose neck.

Drain the beans and stir them into the tomato mixture. Add a little of the cooking liquid from the beans and bring to the boil.

Check the seasoning, add the confit, the gizzards and the goose neck and simmer over a low heat for a further 40 to 50 minutes. Place under the grill for a few minutes before serving.

Note: Goose confit (goose preserved in its own fat), gésiers confits (gizzards similarly preserved) and stuffed goose neck are all specialities of South West France, readily available tinned in France but extremely difficult to find in Britain. Other versions of the traditional cassoulet can be made applying substantially the same method but using other meats.

239

Salt pork with lentils
Petit salé aux lentilles

Serves 6 to 8

Preparation: 20 minutes
Cooking time: 2 1/2-3 hours

Ingredients:

600 g green Puy lentils
1.5 kg mixed salted pork
4-6 sausages
1 bouquet garni
2 onions
Olive oil
Salt, pepper

Wash the pork in cold water. Blanch by placing in cold unsalted water, bring up to simmering point and cook on a low heat for 2 hours. Prick the sausages, add them to the meat and cook for a further 10 minutes.

Pick over and wash the lentils and soak in water for 12 hours. Place in cold, salted water with the onions and bouquet garni. Bring to the boil and simmer for 30 to 40 minutes. (Be careful the water does not boil too vigorously or the lentils will split). When they are done, drain.

Place the salt pork (cut into pieces) and the lentils in a casserole and pour a little of the cooking fluid from the pork over.

Drizzle a little olive oil over, season with pepper, cover and simmer very gently for 20 minutes more.

Serve hot.

Wholewheat spaghetti carbonara
Spaghetti intégral à la carbonara

Serves 4

Preparation: 5 minutes
Cooking time: 5 to 14 minutes

Ingredients:

500 g wholewheat spaghetti
fresh or dried)
8 rashers lean bacon
100 ml crème fraîche
4 eggs
80 g grated parmesan
Salt, pepper

Cook the spaghetti in boiling salted water for 3 minutes if fresh or 12 minutes if dried. Drain and keep warm.

Cut the bacon into small pieces and fry for a few minutes on a high heat. Remove half the fat in the pan, then add the cream and reduce for a few minutes.

Remove from the heat and add the lightly beaten eggs and grated parmesan. Season with salt and pepper, and keep warm.

Serve the pasta at once, with the carbonara sauce poured over.

Suggestions:

Can also be accompanied by a basil sauce or mushroom purée.

Wholewheat tagliatelle with spinach
Tagliatelles intégrales sauce épinards

Serves 6

Preparation: 10 minutes
Cooking time: 20 minutes

Ingredients:

750 g wholewheat tagliatelle (fresh
or dried)
500 g spinach
50 g grated parmesan
2 tablespoons olive oil
200 ml semi-skimmed milk
200 g low-fat crème fraîche
1 egg yolk
1 pinch nutmeg
Salt, pepper

Blanch the spinach in boiling salted water for a few minutes.

Chop the spinach. Over a low heat mix with the olive oil, the crème fraîche, the milk, salt, pepper and nutmeg.

Cook the tagliatelle in boiling salted water for 3 minutes if fresh or about 12 minutes if dried. Drain.

Away from the heat, add the beaten egg yolk to the spinach mixture, stirring well. Pour over the hot tagliatelle and serve.

Turkey thigh with lentil purée
Cuisse de dinde
à la purée de lentilles

Serves 6

Preparation: 15 minutes
Cooking time: 1 hour 15 minutes

Ingredients:

1 turkey thigh (1.2 kg cut into pieces)
200 g smoked bacon
(in a piece, not rashers)
1 onion spiked with a clove
2 shallots
1 clove garlic
25 g low-fat crème fraîche
500 g green lentils
1 bouquet garni (thyme, rosemary, bay)
A few sprigs parsley
1 tablespoon olive oil
Salt, pepper

Soak the lentils in cold water for 12 hours. Dice the bacon and fry in a flame-proof casserole in 1 tablespoon of olive oil, with the sliced shallots.

When the shallots are golden, remove from the casserole and replace with the pieces of turkey. Fry these too until golden brown. Then return the bacon and shallots to the casserole, and add the crushed garlic, the bouquet garni, salt, pepper and three quarters of a litre of water. Simmer on a low heat for 1 hour 15 minutes.

Meanwhile, drain the lentils and cook for 45 minutes on a low heat, in salted (initially cold) water, together with the onion spiked with a clove, pepper and a few bay leaves.

Drain the lentils and put them through the blender, adding a little of the cooking water. Strain through a sieve and add the crème fraîche.

Serve the pieces of turkey accompanied by the lentil purée.

243

Green lentils with tomato and chorizo sausage
Lentilles aux tomates et chorizo

Serves 4 to 6

Preparation: 30 minutes
Cooking time: 1 hour 45 minutes

Ingredients:

500 g green Puy lentils
2 onions
1 clove garlic
2 tablespoons olive oil
250 g chorizo
1 pinch red chilli powder
500 g tomatoes
Chopped parsley
Coarse salt, salt

Soak the lentils in water for 12 hours. Cook in unsalted water (starting from cold) on a low heat for 15 minutes. Add 1 teaspoon coarse salt and cook for 30 minutes more.

In a flame-proof casserole, fry the sliced onion and the crushed garlic. Add the chilli powder, the tomatoes (peeled and quartered) and the chopped parsley.

Season with salt, mingle all the ingredients together quickly and add the chorizo, cut into thin slices. Drain the lentils and pour them into the casserole. Simmer for 15 minutes.

Serve piping hot.

Flageolet beans with button mushrooms
Flageolets aux champignons de Paris

Serves 4

Preparation: 5 minutes
Cooking time: 10 minutes

Ingredients:

1 kg tinned flageolet beans
1 small tin button mushrooms
100 g low-fat crème fraîche
Salt, pepper
Parsley

Drain the flageolet beans and the mushrooms and heat both together on a low heat for 2 to 3 minutes.

Add the crème fraîche, stir and season with salt, pepper and chopped parsley.

Serve at once.

Cheese soufflé
made with wholemeal semolina
Soufflé de semoule
intégrale au fromage

Serves 4

Preparation: 20 minutes
Cooking time: 1 hour 10 minutes

Ingredients:

1 litre milk
6 tablespoons wholemeal semolina
250 g grated gruyère
2 tablespoons olive oil
4 eggs
2 tablespoons parsley
Salt, pepper
Nutmeg

Boil the milk and strew the wholemeal semolina into it, stirring with a spatula while it thickens.

Then add the grated cheese. Season with salt, pepper and nutmeg. Simmer for a further 5 minutes. Beat the egg whites until they form stiff peaks.

Let the semolina cool a little and add the beaten egg yolks, a little at a time, stirring briskly.

Fold in the egg whites and the chopped parsley, mixing the ingredients very gently.

Pour the mixture into an oiled soufflé dish. Place in a gentle oven (150°C, 300°F, gas mark 1-2) for 1 hour.

Serve right away.

DESSERTS

Sultana and fromage frais mould
Flans de fromage
aux raisins secs

(very slight discrepancy)

Serves 6

Preparation: 18 minutes
Cooking time: 25 minutes

Ingredients:

100 g sultanas
250 g fromage frais (40 % fat)
3 eggs
2 leaves (two thirds of sachet)
gelatine
1/2 glass milk
2 tablespoons fructose
1/2 glass rum

The previous day place the sultanas in the rum and leave to swell. If necessary, add a little water so they are completely covered.

Beat the egg yolks and add the fromage frais and the fructose. Beat the egg whites until they form stiff peaks and fold them gently into the mixture.

If using gelatine leaves, soak in cold water to soften, and drain. Heat the milk and add the gelatine. Add the milk to the egg and fromage frais mixture. Drain the sultanas thoroughly and add to the mixture.

Pour into a charlotte mould and cook in the oven at 220°C (gas mark 7) for 25 minutes.

Serve lukewarm or cold.

Lemon and apple creams
Flans au citron et pomme
(very slight discrepancy)

Serves 4

Preparation: 15 minutes
Cooking time: 30 minutes

Ingredients:

4 egg yolks
1 complete egg
3 tablespoons fructose
2 golden delicious apples
(peeled), 400 g
1 1/2 lemons

Beat the egg and the egg yolks together with the fructose. Add the zest of a lemon and the strained juice of 1 lemons.

Grate the apples finely and add to the mixture. Pour into 4 buttered ramekins and cook in a bain-marie at 190°C (375°F, gas mark 5) for 30 minutes.

Turn out and serve lukewarm or cold.

Egg custards
Œufs au lait

(very slight discrepancy)

Serves 5

Preparation: 10 minutes
Cooking time: 30 minutes
Refrigeration: 3 hours

Ingredients:

1/2 litre semi-skimmed milk
5 egg yolks
2 tablespoons fructose
1 vanilla pod

Heat the milk with the vanilla pod, let it cool slightly and remove the vanilla pod.

Beat the egg yolks vigorously and pour the lukewarm milk over. Add the fructose and pour the mixture into ramekins.

Cook in a bain-marie in a moderate oven (180°C, 350°, gas mark 3-4) for about 30 minutes.

Serve cold in the ramekins.

Floating islands
Œufs à la neige

(very slight discrepancy)

Serves 6 to 8

Preparation: 30 minutes
Cooking time: 30 minutes

Ingredients:

1 vanilla pod
8 eggs
1 litre semi-skimmed milk
3 tablespoons fructose
1 pinch salt

Separate the eggs. Beat the whites until they form stiff peaks, adding a pinch of salt.

Boil the milk with the vanilla pod and half a glass of water. Keep it just simmering.

Use a tablespoon to scoop up 'snowballs' of beaten egg white and place on the surface of the milk. Poach them for 1 minute each side, remove and drain on a cloth.

Make an egg custard by beating the egg yolks and adding the lukewarm milk. (Dilute slightly to make the quantity up to 1 litre.) Whisk vigorously.

Place on a low heat again to thicken. Sweeten with the sucrose at the last minute.

Allow to cool. Serve with the 'snowballs' floating on the custard.

Raspberry bavarois
Bavarois aux framboises
(very slight discrepancy)

Serves 4

Preparation: 15 minutes
Refrigeration: 12 hours

Ingredients:

500 g raspberries
1/2 litre milk
4 egg yolks
3 tablespoons fructose
3 leaves (1 sachet) gelatine

Bring the milk to the boil. Beat the egg yolks and fructose together in a large bowl. Gradually pour the milk into the bowl, stirring vigorously all the time.

Return to a low heat and cook until the mixture thickens, stirring continuously. Stir in the gelatine; if using leaves, first soften them in cold water and drain.

Blend 200 g of the raspberries to a purée and combine this with the custard. Add 50 g whole raspberries.

Pour the mixture into ramekins or a charlotte mould and place in the refrigerator for 12 hours to set. Make a raspberry coulis with the remainder of the fruit.

Turn out and serve with the coulis poured over.

Mango bavarois with a kiwi coulis
Bavarois de mangue
au coulis de kiwis

(very slight discrepancy)

Serves 6

Preparation: 15 minutes
Refrigeration: 12 hours

Ingredients:

5 egg yolks
300 ml full cream milk
300 g peeled mango
3 leaves (1 sachet) gelatine
3 tablespoons fructose

For the kiwi coulis:

4 kiwis
Juice of 1 lemon
2 tablespoons fructose

Make an egg custard, as follows. Heat the milk, beat the eggs with the fructose in a large bowl, and gradually pour the milk into the bowl, whisking all the time. Return to a low heat, stirring continuously until the mixture thickens.

Stir in the gelatine; leaves must be previously softened in cold water and drained.

Blend the mango to a smooth purée and stir it into the custard.

Pour the mixture into a mould and leave in the refrigerator to set for 12 hours.

Make a coulis by blending the kiwis with the lemon juice and fructose.

Turn out the bavarois and serve with the kiwi coulis poured over.

Rhubarb bavarois
with a raspberry coulis
Bavarois à la rhubarbe
et son coulis

(very slight discrepancy)

Serves 6

Preparation: 30 minutes
Cooking time: 25 minutes
Refrigeration: 3 hours

Ingredients:

1 kg rhubarb
Juice of 1 lemon
3 leaves (1 sachet) gelatine
100 ml sweet white wine
5 tablespoons fructose
400 g raspberries
3 tablespoon thick low-fat
crème fraîche

Wash and skin the rhubarb and cut into small pieces. Cook in boiling water with the lemon juice for 25 minutes.

Drain the rhubarb and keep the cooking juice. Blend the rhubarb pieces to a fine purée. Stir in the gelatine; leaves must be previously softened in cold water and drained.

Add litre of the cooking juice from the rhubarb, the white wine, the crème fraîche and the sucrose. Combine the ingredients thoroughly, pour into a loaf tin and set in the refrigerator for 3 hours.

Blend the raspberries to make a coulis and strain through a sieve. Serve the bavarois in slices with the raspberry coulis poured over.

Vanilla and chocolate bavarois
Bavarois vanille et chocolat
(very slight discrepancy)

Serves 6

Preparation: 15 minutes
Refrigeration: 12 hours

Ingredients:

750 ml full cream milk
10 egg yolks
5 tablespoons fructose
1 vanilla pod
3 leaves (1 sachet) gelatine
2 teaspoons instant coffee
1 tablespoon rum
150 g dark chocolate with 70 %
minimum cocoa solids

Boil the milk with the vanilla pod (sliced in half lengthways) for 10 minutes.

Dilute the coffee in a few drops of the hot milk. Stir this into the rest of the milk, together with the rum.

Beat the egg yolks with the fructose in a large bowl. Pour the milk into the bowl, stirring continuously. Return to a low heat and stir until the mixture thickens.

Stir in the gelatine; leaves must be previously softened in cold water and drained. Pour the mixture into a mould and set in the refrigerator for 12 hours.

Just before serving, melt the chocolate in a bain-marie, adding a little water. Allow to cool a little. Turn out the bavarois and serve with the lukewarm chocolate poured over.

Apricot mousse. p.259

Floating islands. p.252

Summer fruits mousse, p.257

Mango sorbet. p.260

Crème brûllé. p.268

Summer fruits mousse
Mousse au fromage blanc
et fruits rouges
(very slight discrepancy)

Serves 4 to 5

Preparation: 15 minutes

Ingredients:

250 g fromage frais (20 % fat)
3 egg whites
3 tablespoons fructose
100 g raspberries
100 g small strawberries

Add 1 tablespoon of fructose to the egg whites and beat until they form stiff peaks.

Mix the fromage frais with the other 2 tablespoons of fructose. Fold in the beaten egg whites gently, to make a mousse.

Wash the fruit and cut into pieces. Fold into the mixture.

Place in a large bowl and chill for a few hours.

Grand Marnier mousse
Mousse au grand marnier

(very slight discrepancy)

Serves 4

Preparation: 10 minutes
Refrigeration: 2 hours

Ingredients:

4 eggs
12 petits suisses (30 % fat) or
similar (fromage frais)
3 tablespoons low-fat crème fraîche
40 ml Grand Marnier
3 tablespoons fructose

Beat the egg yolks with the fructose.   Beat the whites until they form stiff peaks.

Combine the petits suisses with the crème fraîche and add the Grand Marnier.   Then add the egg yolks.

Gently fold the egg white into the mixture, to obtain a smooth mousse consistency.

Set in the refrigerator for 2 hours.

Serve chilled.

Apricot mousse
Mousse à l'abricot

(very slight discrepancy)

Serves 4

Preparation: 15 minutes
Refrigeration: 1 hour

Ingredients:

500 g apricots
1 lemon
2 tablespoons fructose
2 leaves (two thirds of sachet) gelatine
150 g fromage frais (20 % fat)
100 g low-fat cream

Blanch the apricots in boiling water for 1 minute. Drain, skin and cut in half to remove the stone.

Blend to a purée and add the lemon juice and the fructose. If using gelatine leaves, soften in cold water and drain. Melt the gelatine in 2 tablespoons water in a bain-marie and immediately combine with the apricot purée.

Whip the fromage frais and add to the mixture, combining thoroughly.

Pour the mousse into ramekins and set in the refrigerator for 3 hours.

Serve well chilled.

Mango sorbet
Sorbet à la mangue

(very slight discrepancy)

Serves 4

Preparation: 10 minutes
Refrigeration: 3 hours

Ingredients:

2 ripe mangoes (providing
450 g flesh)
1 small tin of condensed
unsweetened semi-skimmed milk
2 tablespoons lemon juice
A few drops vanilla essence
2 tablespoons fructose

Peel and stone the mangoes and chop the flesh into small pieces.

Blend with the concentrated milk, the lemon juice, vanilla essence and fructose (the consistency should be light and frothy).

Place the mousse in the freezer for about 3 hours. Use a scoop to serve, as if it were ice-cream.

Recommendation:

Use a sorbet-maker for best results.

Baked summer fruits dessert
Gratin de fruits rouges

(very slight discrepancy)

Serves 8

Preparation: 10 minutes
Cooking time: 25 to 30 minutes

Ingredients:

750 g strawberries
750 g raspberries
5 eggs
1/2 litre semi-skimmed milk
200 ml low-fat crème fraîche
4 tablespoons fructose

Cut the strawberries in half. In a gratin dish place alternately layers of strawberries and raspberries, with each layer separated by a thin layer of crème fraîche. Finish with a layer of raspberries.

Lightly beat the eggs and add the milk and fructose. Pour the mixture over the fruit and bake at 200°C (400°F, gas mark 6) for 25 to 30 minutes.

Serve lukewarm or cold.

261

Whipped cream Nata
Crème chantilly Nata

(very slight discrepancy) [1]

Serves 4

Preparation: 15 minutes

Ingredients:

25 cl whipping cream
Vanilla essence

Put the cream and the bowl in which you are going to whip it in the freezer for 30 minutes.

Use an electric whisk to whip the cream until it is stiff (but be careful not to over-whip and turn it to butter).

Before it is finished, add 2 or 3 drops of vanilla essence, whipping continuously.

Place in the refrigerator and serve with summer fruits (strawberries, raspberries, redcurrants, blackberries).

Suggestions:

You can also add 1 or 2 tablespoons dark chocolate powder (Van Houten or similar) towards the end, when the cream is almost whipped.

In hot weather, whip the cream with the bowl placed in a larger one containing ice cubes.

Note:
This dessert comes into the 'very slight discrepancy category because, although the vanilla essence contains a very small amount of sugar, the whipped cream usually accompanies strawberries and raspberries, whose sugar (fructose) content is extremely low.

Strawberries or raspberries 'Nata' are therefore the best dessert to have in Phase II and the only one you can allow yourself to indulge in from time to time in Phase I.

Wholemeal pancakes
Pâte à crêpes intégrale
(slight discrepancy)

Makes 15 pancakes

Preparation: 10 minutes
Cooking time: 3 minutes per pancake

Ingredients:

250 g wholemeal flour (T 202)
1/2 litre semi-skimmed milk
2 eggs
1 teaspoon sunflower oil
1 pinch salt
(orange flower water for dessert pancake)

Put the wholemeal flour in a large mixing-bowl. Make a well in the centre and break the eggs into it.

Add a pinch of salt and mix gently with a whisk, pouring in the milk a little at a time. Then add the sunflower oil (and orange flower water if used), combine the ingredients thoroughly and leave to rest for 2 hours in the refrigerator.

When you are about to make the pancakes, add a little water or milk to the mixture to be sure it is runny enough.

Cook in a non-stick pan.

Suggestions:

This pancake mixture is suitable for all kinds of fillings, whether savoury or sweet, but remember sweet fillings must be made with fructose.

Chocolate wholemeal cream
Crème pâtissière intégrale au chocolat

(slight discrepancy)

Serves 4 to 5

Preparation: 10 minutes
Cooking time: 20 minutes

Ingredients:

1 litre semi-skimmed milk
6 eggs
100 g wholemeal flour
150 g dark chocolate with 70 % minimum cocoa solids
40 g fructose

Boil the milk. Lightly beat the eggs and add the sieved flour a little at a time.

Let the milk cool a little. Pour into the mixture, whipping vigorously all the time. Return to a low heat until the mixture is creamy, stirring continuously. Cook for 3 minutes.

Melt the chocolate in a bain-marie and add it to the mixture. Add the fructose and combine thoroughly. Serve tepid or cold. (Stir the cream from time to time while it is cooling.)

Chocolate soufflé
Soufflé au chocolat

(slight discrepancy)

Serves 6

Preparation: 15 minutes
Cooking time: 20 minutes

Ingredients:

200 g dark chocolate with 70 %
minimum cocoa solids
5 eggs
40 ml milk
25 g single cream
A few drops lemon juice

Preheat the oven to 190°C (375°F, gas mark 5). Break the chocolate into pieces and melt in a bain-marie. Away from the heat, add the milk, cream, and egg yolks, stirring continuously with a whisk.

Add the lemon juice to the egg whites and beat until they form stiff peaks. Fold gently into the chocolate mixture, a little at a time.

Butter a 17 centimetre soufflé mould and pour the mixture into it. Cook in the oven, turned down to the lowest setting, for 20 minutes.

Serve immediately so that the soufflé does not collapse.

Chocolate mousse
Mousse au chocolat
(slight discrepancy)

Serves 6 to 8

Preparation: 25 minutes
Cooking time: 10 minutes
Refrigeration: 5 hours

Ingredients:

400 g dark chocolate with 70 %
minimum cocoa solids
8 eggs
1/2 glass rum (70 ml)
4 teaspoons instant coffee
1 pinch salt

Break the chocolate into pieces and place in a bain-marie. Make half a cup of very strong coffee and add to the chocolate, together with the rum.

Melt the chocolate in the bain-marie, stirring with a spatula.

Separate the eggs and beat the whites, with a pinch of salt added, until they form stiff peaks.

Allow the chocolate to cool down a little in a large bowl and add the egg yolks, stirring briskly. Gently fold in the beaten egg whites, a little at a time, to obtain a smooth mousse.

Allow to set in the refrigerator for at least 5 hours before serving.

Suggestion:

The addition of orange zest will add a delightful flavour to this mousse.

Rich chocolate dessert
Moelleux au chocolat

(slight discrepancy)

Serves 4

Preparation: 20 minutes
Cooking time: 10 minutes

Ingredients:

250 g dark chocolate with 70 %
minimum cocoa solids
5 eggs
1/2 glass milk
1 pinch salt

Melt 200 g of the chocolate in a bain-marie with the half-glass of milk. Separate the eggs. Beat the whites, adding a pinch of salt, until they form stiff peaks. Add the yolks, beating continuously with an electric whisk until the mixture is smooth.

Add this mixture to the chocolate, still in the bain-marie. Stir continuously until the mixture turns thick and 'lumpy' (as the eggs cook, the mixture will shrink in volume and will take on a consistency like scrambled eggs).

Transfer the mixture to a cake tin or shallow dish which will allow for it to be spread to 2cm deep, and allow to cool a little.

Meanwhile, melt the remaining 50 g of dark chocolate in a bain-marie, with 4 or 5 tablespoons of water. When it is completely melted, pour over the cake, spreading it like icing, using a spatula.

This rich chocolate dessert can be eaten right away, lukewarm, or cold after 1 hour in the refrigerator. It can also be eaten with whipped cream.

Recommendation:

If you keep it in the fridge for a while, remove 2 hours before serving.

Crème brûlée

(slight discrepancy)

Serves 4 or 5

Preparation: 20 minutes
Cooking time: 1 1/2 hours
Refrigeration: 3 hours

Ingredients:

6 egg yolks
50 g fructose
2 teaspoons vanilla essence
120 ml full cream milk
200 g thick crème fraîche

Beat the egg yolks with a hand whisk, and add the fructose. Continue until the mixture grows pale.

Bring the milk to the boil with the vanilla essence. Remove from the heat immediately and allow to cool for a few minutes.

Add the milk to the egg yolks. Add the cream and stir in gently.

Pour the mixture into four ramekins. Cook in a slow oven (90°C, 200°F, gas mark) for 1 hours. Leave to cool before placing in the refrigerator.

Before serving, sprinkle the surface with fructose and place under the grill for a few moments to brown the top or use a blowlamp.

Suggestions:

It is possible to add summer fruits to this mixture.

IDEAS FOR A MONTIGNAC PARTY

IDEAS FOR A MONTIGNAC PARTY

The worst fear of anyone who has adopted the principles of the 'Method', is to find himself or herself at a traditional party, which usually means an occasion where little sandwiches and canapés made with white bread vie for space with vol-au-vents and miniature pizzas.

Add to these the 'super-sweetened' petits fours and the elaborate centrepiece which the pastrycook has lovingly stuck together with caramelised sugar and you have what it takes to drive even the least rigid Montignac enthusiast to despair.

In my earlier books I gave some brief advice which should enable you to avoid coming adrift completely, particularly when you are in Phase I.

Of course the ideal situation would be to persuade professional caterers to mend their ways, to force them out of the sandwich routine and get them to produce acceptable party titbits.

Plenty of people who have deliberately broken with convention have managed to find a thousand and one original ideas to grace their party buffet.

There is no limit to the inventive possibilities; indeed, so many variations and combinations are possible that your imagination has all the scope you could want.

Here are some basic ingredients you can use to dream up a 'Montignac buffet'. Over to you to put them together as you see fit!

Vegetables:

> – cucumber
> – celery
> – mushrooms

- leeks
- asparagus
- artichoke hearts
- salsify
- hearts of palm
- chicory
- radishes
- cauliflower
- gherkins
- tomatoes, cherry tomatoes
- sweet peppers
- any green salad ingredients

Eggs:

- slices of hard-boiled egg
- pigeons 'or quails' eggs
- fish roe

Cheeses:

- Emmental
- Gouda
- Cheddar
- feta
- mozzarella
- Roquefort
- soft cheeses with herbs

Cooked meats:

- sausages
- slicing sausage
- garlic sausage
- cooked ham
- raw ham
- foie gras

Fish and seafood:

- shrimps
- mussels

- scampi
- tuna
- crab
- smoked salmon
- fish sticks
- herring
- smoked fish (haddock, trout)

Poultry:

- chicken breasts
- magret de canard (smoked duck breast)
- roast turkey

Cold meat:

- roast veal
- roast beef
- roast pork

When it comes to desserts, you can simply make miniature versions of the ones suggested in the recipe section.

CONCLUSION

The recipes set out in this book comply with the simple principles which underlie the MONTIGNAC Method, namely:

– choosing carbohydrates of low or very low glycaemic index, notably food rich in fibre.

– giving preference to monounsaturated fats (such as olive oil and goose fat), or balancing out the good and bad types of fat within a given recipe (by using, for example, olive oil with crème fraîche).

– excluding refined foods:

• white flours (replaced in sauces by mushroom purée).

• sugar (replaced by the sweet flavours of fruits or, occasionally, by fructose).

• white rice, non-wholewheat pasta and semolina (replaced by their wholegrain or wholemeal equivalents).

– excluding potatoes, sweetcorn and carrots, because of their very high glycaemic index.

– resorting occasionally to gelatine (a protein which is nutritionally neutral) in making bavarois or terrines.

The book could as well have been written by any number of readers who, over a period of time, have completely mastered the nutritional principles of the MONTIGNAC Method.

RECIPES PHASE I

STARTERS

Soups

Moulds and terrines

Crudités

Salads

Eggs

Fish and seafood

MAIN COURSE

Eggs

Meat

Poultry and game

Fish and seafood

ACCOMPANYING VEGETABLES

CARBOHYDRATE DISHES

RECIPES PHASE II

STARTERS

MAIN COURSE

DESSERTS with VERY SLIGHT DISCREPANCY

DESSERTS with SLIGHT DISCREPANCY

CONTENTS

285

Printed in Great Britain by J. H. Haynes & Co. Ltd.